Praise for Success to Die for

"This groundbreaking book will set the standard for this subject. Previously unexplored areas are now unearthed, changing the way we perceive women in the role of entrepreneurship. We now can face these issues head on and work together to solve these rarely discussed areas. Thank you, Lynette, for presenting this delicate subject in a manner where people will understand and want to be more proactive"

-Colleen Brigid Fitzpatrick, MSW, LCSW, owner of Instrumental Change, LLC

"Compelling and engaging book honestly addressing the challenges, successes, joys and pains of being a businesswoman. These pains and challenges are exacerbated by mental health concerns as well as by the realities of balancing life and business. Ms. Davis offers insights into leadership and how women can exhibit nurturing and account-able leadership for themselves and others. For example, as a means of demonstrative leadership Ms. Davis speaks of using our available platforms to heal ourselves and propagate important messages. This is a book about strength, confidence, and self-love."

-Paloma Amar Coleman, PsyD., principal consultant of EAC Leadership Consulting, LLC

Ms. Davis, a long standing mental health activist and entrepreneur, speaks openly and frankly about her own battles with anxiety and depression. Through sharing her own story and those of other women like her, Davis challenges the cultural stigma that attempts to alienate and silence people that "do not fit the norm." The truth is that none of us fit the norm. We all battle with feelings of insecurity, unworthiness, fear, and perfectionism. However, by observing the lives of these courageous business owners, we learn that we are not broken and we are not alone. The strategies that these women embody equips them with a "roller coaster resilience" that is available to us all.

-Dr. Kesha Moore, founder of Life In Focus Coaching and author of *Your Life as a Celebration*

"AMAZING!"

"Finally, a book that drops pretension, goes beyond the quick fix formulas for "how to create a successful business" and tells us the truth. Davis, offers a unique, well researched and compassionate guide for entrepreneurs starting out and those who have been at it awhile. With humor, frankness and hope, Davis explores the inner reality so many of us grasp with, hidden from view: shame, depression, despair and pain. Then, she suggests through entrepreneurship we can find wholeness, despite the pain of the journey--however, first we must examine the links between mental and emotional health inside of the world of business and the issues that arise because of it. Davis is a fresh voice calling for a paradigm shift in how we show up and why it's life or death, if we don't change it now."

-Jardana Peacock, director of Liberation School and author of *Practice Showing Up*

"Lynette Davis is a brave woman. Many hear the call but never answer it, within themselves, much less more publicly. But in writing this book, Lynette has answered the call in both ways, daring to tell her own story of struggle with mental health and entrepreneurship and giving voice and a platform to other women to do the same. In doing so, Lynette shines a light for any woman who isn't sure she's enough, or that she should continue to pursue a dream, or whose negative beliefs lead her to the conclusion that she's too broken to be successful. At one point in her preface, Lynette says she " found hope, strength, and connection" in every narrative. I think in reading *Success to Die For* you'll find the same."

- Anastacia Brice, founder of AssistU

"Every businesswoman should read *Success to Die For*, and so should the people who care for them. In the twenty-five years I've been serving as a business coach for women entrepreneurs, I've heard from my clients over and over stories just like the ones Lynette Davis shares. Some of these stories I've lived through myself. Entrepreneurship is a tough road for anyone, and often even tougher for women. If you add to that burden a history of mental health issues, running a business can feel like climbing a mountain every day. This intelligent and insightful book will show you that you're not alone in your struggle, and that anxiety and depression don't have to stop you from having a successful business and a fulfilling life."

-C.J. Hayden, author of *Get Clients Now!*

"The unique challenges facing women entrepreneurs extend far beyond the well-established issues of unequal startup financing. Businesswomen must also find ways to thrive in a world that expects perfection and 24/7 hustle while denying the reality of mental illness. In *Success to Die For*, Lynette Davis unpacks the cultural expectations that are keeping female entrepreneurs unhappy, unhealthy, and unable to enjoy their successes. Davis's ability to hold a compassionate mirror to the mental health problems plaguing businesswomen will help you to take a closer look at what you are giving up in the pursuit of "success." *Success to Die For* will show you how to center love in your business and your life so that you can succeed without sacrificing your mental health and stability."

-Emily Guy Birken, author of *End Financial Stress Now*

Success to
Die For

Success to Die For

BREAKING DOWN ASSUMPTIONS
ABOUT ANXIETY, DEPRESSION,
& SUICIDE AND THEIR IMPACT
ON BUSINESS WOMEN

Lynette Davis

Success to die for: Breaking down assumptions about anxiety, depression, & suicide and their impact on business women

Copyright © 2017 Lynette Davis

Some events are out of chronological order to protect identities of real persons.

This book is not intended to be a substitute for the medical advice of a licensed medical professional. The reader should consult with their doctor in any matters relating to her/his health.

Cover design and illustrations by Susan Krupp
Editing by Pamela Barroway
Author photograph by Jeff Lek
Book design by CreateSpace

Davis, Lynette.
Success to die for: Breaking down assumptions about anxiety, depression, & suicide and their impact on business women / Lynette Davis

ISBN-13: 9781974608911
ISBN-10: 1974608913
Library of Congress Control Number: 2017913000
CreateSpace Independent Publishing Platform
North Charleston, South Carolina

Visit www.loveselflovebiz.com

Disclaimer

book. You should also ask your physician or other healthcare provider to assist you in interpreting any information in this book or in the referenced websites, or applying the information to your individual case.

If you believe you have a medical emergency, or if you are worried that you or someone you know may be at risk for suicide, please call your physician, the National Suicide Prevention Lifeline at 1-800-273-8255 or local authorities (such as 911) immediately.

Dedication

*For my very first teachers, who encouraged
me to speak and live my truth:
my mother, Lavern, and my grandmother, Ingrid.*

*In honor of the women (and a few men)
who had the courage to share their truths for this book.*

Contents

Preface

———

LESS THAN TWO HUNDRED BUCKS and a dream. Two wide-eyed and somewhat desperate twenty-somethings who had absolutely no clue what they were taking on decided to go the entrepreneurial route and start a business. We were both unemployed, job prospects were … well, let's just say thousands in student loan debt – for a degree that others jokingly said only offered a chance to say "would you like fries with that" – was quite debilitating. So, we forked over the last of our savings to create an opportunity to be useful in a society that constantly rejected us. About a year into our far-from-financially-successful endeavor, my business partner decided she had sacrificed too much and it was time to find a job; she handed the company over to me.

Because the business was my brainchild, I was encouraged by my mentors to go at it alone rather than seek out another business partner. Trusted mentors knew I struggled with confidence issues, but optimistically believed (with time and experience) I'd overcome those issues. What none of us knew was that I was barely holding on; I had been triggered (i.e. anxiety) and it would set the stage for how my business progressed going forward. Still, I acted on their advice, full of anxiety and not believing a darn word anyone said about my so-called potential. Meanwhile, I was hurt and growing angry at my friend, and former business partner for abandoning our company before we even had the chance to get wings and fly. This reaction was truly a reflection of the fear within myself for believing that I chased her away like I seemingly did with everyone else. In a pattern of downward-spiraling conclusions, my mantra was that I had it coming – after all, I somehow made it about myself, and because of that I wasn't worthy of the success in any form. Since I couldn't seem to get "adulting" right, I easily settled into those thoughts for the next few years … struggling with the belief that something was inherently wrong with me. Self-fulfilling my belief system of unworthiness in how I showed up in my life, including my work.

Despite this deep-seated negative belief system, I wore my mask like many do in order to "fake it until you make it." Because I was busy keeping myself busy, however, I wasn't aware of donning this mask and as a result buried my angst. All the while the world kept turning and both my former business partner and I suffered in silence.

Not too long after she made a healthy decision to walk away from the business in an effort to find balance, I received a call from one of her spiritual mentors. This person informed me that my former business partner – who had become a sister-like friend – had intended death by suicide, but for whatever reason didn't go through with the attempt and decided to check herself into an inpatient mental health hospital for treatment. I cried while listening, cried after hanging up, and cried on the way to visit her before plastering on my brave face. I mean, for goodness sake, my friend, was ready to file a permanent cease-and-desist report on the physical property that housed her soul! And I couldn't help! I couldn't do a darn thing about it. I felt so powerless and incapable; I couldn't even begin to imagine what was going on in her mind … at least, that's what I initially told myself.

After I received that gut-wrenching phone call, a seed planted long before began to take root, and many questions, worries, doubts, and speculations began to form and consumed many of my waking thoughts. So, I did the only thing I knew how to do: picked up the phone and reached out.

I spoke with mental health professionals, sought research, called friends to tell them I loved them just in case no one else did. Once my friend began her mental health recovery journey, I saw her in a new light. She became my she-hero, and I realized everyday "sheroes" live ordinary lives with extraordinary courage. And they need their tales told too – otherwise, who would know about their incredible bravery, resilience, and determination taking place in the battlefields of their minds?

After a lot of encouragement, I eventually reached out to colleagues, fellow home-based business owners like myself, "mom and pop" shop owners, start-up founders bustling about in the Silicon Valley, and side business hustlers who worked full-time in leading positions. Most of the content presented in this book is gathered from these many social media behavioral observations, interviews, quick instant message chats, and spontaneous surveys. The more I spoke to colleagues about the issues I was too ashamed to admit I had while attempting to build a business, the more I learned just how many individuals from "millennials" to "the silent generation" shared similar experiences – same-engine vehicles just with different paint jobs. I decided to put my sociology degree to use and tackle a very "close to home" research project.

I was gifted with a chance to listen to very sad and deeply personal narratives from colleagues, business friends, and "recovery family" members about their loved ones who, in some cases, had died by suicide before intervention was even a possibility. I heard accounts of individuals wanting to give up on some days while wishing so very badly to "be the change." I listened in as people spoke of achieving great financial success yet feeling deluded, empty, and unfulfilled. I listened as people recalled how downtrodden they'd become due to lack of adequate finances. Yet despite the dark topic matter, within every narrative I found hope, strength, and connection.

Perhaps seeking to "hold space" with others made a difference, perhaps there was something more, but I knew that I wanted to truly live and not just *exist* anymore … and, moreover, I wanted others to feel the same. I wanted to encourage all of us to live on, to believe in ourselves, to return to love, stand in our power, and to give this world a much-needed mental wellness makeover. Maybe I was a bit idealistic and high-strung – I am entrepreneurial, after all – but I wanted to move forward and show up … anxiety and all.

True to my personality, I then began to worry that potential readers would ask "why should I read this book?" and just "who do you think you are?" Well, I could describe my professional background working the mean streets of urban cities New Jersey as a social services worker in the substance abuse field. (Ever try driving a crack addict to rehab?) I could go on about the mental health courses I completed, my support group facilitating experience, and how I've helped at-risk youth achieve personal goals despite traumatic life events during my time as a behavioral health mentor. I could talk forever about the many years of problem-solving and freedom engineering experience I gained working as a right-hand woman to licensed clinicians, counselors, and coaches just to prove that I've worked on both the direct care "in the trenches" side of mental health *and* the administrative side. I could also talk about my collaborations with medical professionals from prestigious universities while writing this book in order to offer you a scholarly perspective. My passion and heart for this topic is probably obvious, and I've learned much about coping strategies from my own personal experiments with treatment and recovery as someone who has a history of anxiety and depression.

And while I think all of the above were worth mentioning, none of these points really defines me. At the heart of mental health activism and advocacy are many individuals doing what they can to create awareness, decrease stigma, and even come up with creative solutions to systemic problems. I am requesting your precious time because I believe that if picking up this book, you too have a notion swirling around in your head that somehow, in some way, you can change the world – starting with tending to your own mental wellness and the health of your business.

I also believe that in order to change our perception of reality we have to come face-to-face with our truths … no matter how darn ugly those facts may seem. Isn't that why we break down assumptions, because in understanding truth we are set free? Free to be the change, the exception, and the legacy creator with our newfound awareness?

I know that you as a leader, entrepreneur, and influencer can be a catalyst for amazing change in the lives of those you encounter, just by showing up and being true to yourself. Within this book you will find words to reignite a fiery passion or spark the determination to keep moving toward that "somehow, someway" as it calls to you from a place of deep meaning and purpose.

So here I am, vulnerable and courageously writing to you as a woman and business owner wanting to add to a conversation already taking place while specifically addressing the experiences of other women who are also entrepreneurs and/or business owners dealing with mental illness. I honestly believe we owe it to ourselves and the generations to come to pay attention to the battle cries of "sheroes," warrior women, or as Jungian psychoanalyst, Dr. Clarissa Pinkola Estés posits in her work, *Women Who Run with the Wolves,*[1] those who fight every day to thrive in ways beyond imagination.

Beyond sharing personal narratives, this book offers insight and resources for understanding the intimate relationship between mental health concerns, entrepreneurship, and the ongoing grind of running a sustainable business. I attempt to explain why it is important to understand the relationship, and share some examples of using this knowledge to the benefit of workplace culture and society as a whole. As a result of my investigation into this topic, I introduce to some – and perhaps, present to others – some evidence-based practices for building what I've come to term "roller-coaster resilience" for the often-bumpy ride that is entrepreneurship and business ownership. None of these suggested practices are an absolute "right way" of doing or being. My intention is not to present one idea over another as if either were the holy grail of mental wellness. I do my best to present what I've found through research that both resonated with me and happened to also be common themes among interviewees.

In this book, I strive to avoid coming across extra scholarly, or imply that what you read is "no earthly good"; my approach is to be down-to-earth and accessible to readers from many different walks of life (hence the pop culture references). I'm confident I came pretty close to accomplishing a practical read that is concise and yet provocatively telling.

Ultimately, my desire is to see you receive added value on understanding mental health implications through a psychosocial looking glass, and with compassion accept perceived shortcomings as a call to action. A dare of sorts, to pick up where I leave off, to share your story whether through content or company policies; which, in turn, invites your sphere of influence to add to this movement toward mental health concerns being recognized, destigmatized, and adequately addressed in the workplace and in life. *This* is my starting point.

Introduction

—◆—

THE INITIAL QUESTION WAS SIMPLE and perhaps not so uncommon: Could we be more productive and truly have a business and life we love despite mental health issues?

The question came to me after I read a quote by the late Aaron Swartz, who was an internet activist in the tech scene: "I have a lot of illnesses. I don't talk about it much, for a variety of reasons. I feel ashamed to have an illness. It sounds absurd, but there still is an enormous stigma around being sick – but I don't want to use being ill as an excuse. (Although I sometimes wonder how much more productive I'd be if I wasn't so sick.)". Swartz concluded that he didn't find the subject interesting enough to think about it further.[2]

Because Aaron and other entrepreneurs like him have died by suicide, or have attempted to, I not only found the subject interesting, I became deeply engrossed by it. With the cookie crumb trail laid down, I decided to go ahead and follow my curiosity about situations not only directly affecting my own life and work, but also – as I learned – so many others in business too. Because this happened in the STEM (science, technology, engineering, and mathematics) startup arena, I started investigating there and found myself trading emails and reading about, or listening to, accounts of male founders who had begun being unapologetically vocal about mental health issues in the Silicon Valley. Some had also lost both female and male colleagues to suicide. While more men were coming out about their mental illnesses, most notably after they achieved certain success factors, this didn't seem to be the case for women in the same industry. While wanting to understand why that was so, I didn't want to limit my scope to startups – especially as someone from a nonprofit background who primarily worked with and had the most access to service-based solopreneurs. So, I branched out.

Understanding what lies beneath the roles we play and the masks we wear.

One of many things I learned from years of working behind the scenes with counselors and life/business coaches, was that women in particular held themselves back due to mental blockage that translated into behavioral patterns affecting business growth … hence a reason for seeking out coaches.

However, this "blockage" seemed a bit complicated. I couldn't help but wonder, *why* did we hold ourselves back? Was this a form of self-fulfilling prophesy or is someone – unnoticed – pulling invisible strings and puppeteering? If there were indeed factors outside of ourselves triggering and making us unwell, then why did we feel ashamed about illness? I also wondered why we would rather toss aside understanding and speaking our truth in favor of suffering in silence and putting up "everything is awesome" facades.

So, I dug a little deeper – starting with myself and my self-sabotaging perceptions. Where some people saw opportunity in the "free world," I saw established systems long ago built to keep opportunity at bay and the resulting sense of overwhelming defeat and disenchantment. Not believing in myself, however, was only a part of my story. I saw that no matter where I tried to "fake it till I made it," I couldn't blend in or fit the mold, and so was constantly reminded that I didn't belong or was 'other'; I couldn't shake feeling that I was an imposter on more levels than one. Why, I always wondered, did I feel that way? And how I could mend the brokenness inside to see things in a new light?

It's been written that one should: "Always remember that you are absolutely unique. Just like everyone else."[3] I've had enough life experience to know that while my thoughts and feelings felt individualistic, certain circumstances can be felt at a societal level. I speculated, who else identified with feeling like they're "other"? How much of that feeling was the basis for debilitating health issues? And was entrepreneurship the pathway for "others" like myself to find a place to belong? What common thread could I write about with my whole heart while offering you, the reader, solace through a collaborated effort? To confidently tell you that while those feelings of "otherness," shame, and defeat were valid, they didn't fully represent our truth – and also that despite our perceptions, we could begin to transform our thinking, behaviors, and even change up the game? I couldn't even begin to address those questions without reaching out and connecting with other women in business. Women who were also ready to understand themselves, to dig deep to find and speak their own truths.

PROTECTING THE IDENTITIES OF MY INVESTIGATION PARTICIPANTS.

By promising to preserve anonymity, I was able to persuade women leaders from the United States, Canada, England, and Australia to answer my written surveys or hop onto one-on-one interview calls. As such, I use their initials if quoting directly or the pseudonyms "Amaya," "Willow," "Eleanor," "Tia," and "Jane" to represent responses so similar in nature that combining them together as one main point of reference made the most sense.

A QUICK NOTE ABOUT TERMINOLOGY.

In the field of mental health there is a fixation on terminology. Because I'm choosing not to focus on any one point of view, however, I will interchangeably use terms like mental health disorder, mental illness, mental health concern, mental health issues, etc. to essentially say that which is *opposite of mental wellness*. According to the World Health Organization (WHO), mental wellness or mental health is defined as "a state of well-being in which the individual realizes his or her own abilities, can cope with the normal stresses of life, can work productively and fruitfully, and is able to make a contribution to his or her community."[4]

Furthermore, I think it's important to acknowledge that – terms aside – the ultimate goal of mental health advocates such as myself is to contribute to the transformation of an opposite of mental wellness *into mental wellness* for ourselves and one another.

WHAT I'VE LEARNED FROM TRUTH DIGGING.

The stepping stones toward transformation start with awareness and acknowledgement. After all, how can we change what we refuse to see plainly or stubbornly deny the existence of?

When considering the process of transformation in terms of entrepreneurship and/or running a business, the words "I sometimes wonder how much more productive I'd be if I wasn't so sick" always resurfaced. Only I thought to address the issue culturally: how much more productive could we be if we didn't suppress the means for being well? Specifically, I asked this question of those who self-reported having been diagnosed with mental illness at one point in their lives, because I wanted to know (and I want you to know) their truths so you will understand you are not alone.

Finally, I decided to explore the personal narratives of entrepreneurial women because they set the stage for the culture of their work environments while simultaneously being a part of social structures that have historically been set by men. Because social norms influence so much of how we live, work, and even play, what blocked us from truly being the superheroines of our own life stories and in turn our businesses? Was mental wellness in the workplace possible despite the root causes of mental health disarray? How do success stories of women business owners with mental illness unfold and which resources could help better position those still struggling along the way? My attempt at unearthing answers to those questions, and what was revealed, became the subsequent chapters of this book.

CHAPTER 1

To the Extraordinary Ones, Cheers!

—◆—

Here's to the crazy ones, the misfits, the rebels, the troublemakers, the round pegs in the square holes... the ones who see things differently – they're not fond of rules... You can quote them, disagree with them, glorify or vilify them, but the only thing you can't do is ignore them because they change things... they push the human race forward, and while some may see them as the crazy ones, we see genius, because the ones who are crazy enough to think that they can change the world, are the ones who do.

– Rob Siltanen, "Crazy Ones" from the Apple "Think Different" advertisement, 1997

"Mental Health Disorder and Successful Entrepreneur." Sounds like a true conundrum, doesn't it? Yet, as I collected psychological studies on the topic, conducted one-to-one interviews with female entrepreneurs, freelancers, and small/large business owners, and even reached out to the men who partnered with them, I found the two subjects went together quite often … and about as a well as a popsicle on a hot summer day.

There seems to be a general consensus that it takes a special personality to become an entrepreneur. Entrepreneurs are known to be impulsive, risk-taking in a way other personality types aren't, and very passionate. A common thread is that they are essentially looking to achieve success; however, this success is to be realized on their own terms. While entrepreneurs are quick to make mantras out of phrases like "fail fast," they don't wake up and yell out in their best Prince Akeem *Coming To America* voice,[5] "I can't wait to start a business that's going to leave me penniless!" So that we're on the same page, Merriam-Webster defines success as: "the fact of getting or achieving wealth, respect, or fame."[6] Great! We're all on a mission to get lots of money, minions, and make multiple appearances on anything hosted by Oprah, media proprietor extraordinaire.

Well, I don't know about you, but the conventional definition of success feels a bit incomplete. And after years of researching and personally asking colleagues and mentors from around the world to share their personal definition of success, some – definitions of which I'll share in Chapter 3 – I can say that their definitions were much more colorful and broader than Merriam-Webster's.

All the wealth, all the respect, and all the fame in the universe does not prevent us from feeling like our worlds are caving in on us or like we're suffocating and alone. I think it may be safe to propose a theory that debilitating feelings of chronic suffering make us not as successful as one might perceive.

So, I wondered if perhaps having these specific personality traits bottled up would make one more susceptible to mental disorders. Or if people susceptible to mental illness would be more likely to choose to become entrepreneurs. Turns out I wasn't the only one with this train of thought.

In 1993, Johns Hopkins professor and author Kay Redfield Jamison, Ph.D., wrote *Touched with Fire,* which explored the correlation between manic-depressive illness (most of us know this by the current terminology, bipolar) and the artistic temperament. She points to the notion that linking "madness and genius" has been an ongoing and quite controversial endeavor.[7] More recently another author, Nassir Ghaemi, M.D., wrote the 2012 *A First-Rate Madness: Uncovering the Links Between Leadership and Mental Illness* that explored the powerful connections between mental illness and leadership.[8]

Michael Freeman, M.D. saw that there was plenty of research around the personality traits of successful entrepreneurs, but noticed that little was known about their mental health characteristics. Deciding to dig in, Dr. Freeman collaborated with colleagues at the University of California, Berkeley in a 2015 study called *Are Entrepreneurs "Touched with Fire?"* The study's results indeed "suggest an underlying relationship between entrepreneurship and many of the affective, cognitive, and behavioral differences associated with mental health conditions".[9] With this knowledge in hand, the next logical questions to ask are: why does this type of relationship exist, and does it help or hurt us – entrepreneurs and society alike?

Dr. Freeman and his team of researchers led me to believe that it made sense to go beyond the basic understanding of mental health issues among entrepreneurs – which is, of course, a necessary exercise in removing barriers keeping us from being successful in an authentic, well-rounded, and wholehearted way. But we must also strive to develop "proactive, protective, and accessible resources" for business owners to not feel so broken along the way that they take their own lives and not finish their enterprising journeys.[10]

THE GAME OF LIFE AND WORK-RELATED STRESS.
Now just wait a moment! How did I go from saying "successful entrepreneur," even if diagnosed with a mental illness, to wanting resources and aid for suicide prevention?

As I mentioned earlier, the entrepreneurial lifestyle is typically categorized as a sort of "daredevil" lifestyle full of risks – namely, financial risks. So, it should be no surprise that individuals venturing out to create opportunities for themselves, others, and even the world may do so using their last dime.

According to research presented by the Money and Mental Health Policy Institute, people who have had a "major financial crisis" within the past six months are nearly eight times more likely to experience suicidal thoughts.[11] Business hazards, indeed.

Books like *$100 Startup* provide snapshots of entrepreneurs who start with a very minimal investment and move on to their triumphant empire-building crusades and the daring tale of how they made a dollar out of fifteen cents and lived happily ever after, the end (or rich and unhappily ever after). Some of the stories briefly describe how these individuals failed miserably and drank the last of their nickels and dimes away before a strategic regroup; but then the narrative goes back to the "and now they're the owner of such and such, a multi-million-dollar enterprise"![12] Amazing! Such tales gives us the hopes and aspirations that if they can, we can too … even if statistics tell us otherwise. But I want to backpedal a bit and talk about the failure story and spotlight the "downfall" because this is where the link between mental illness and money meet. This is where we now have an opportunity to step into a space of healing, character development, empathetic listening, coping skills, and resilience building.

So even though a failure often feels like the end, I believe breakdowns are often the beginning. A very crucial moment where a person not only can take and apply lessons for their own life going forward, but also take and apply life lessons as a way to give back on a much larger and systemic scale. This is an opportunity to see "giving back" as much more than altruistic charity, but a time and a place to change the rules of the game.

"Game changers" in the truest sense are those who take many communities to higher heights. Game changers are the ones who challenge totally broken systems, or systems that have failed enough people to cause a stir in the atmosphere. Considering the ever-increasing number of business owners, I decided to focus on a very specific and growing segment in the entrepreneurial landscape: women who are game changers.

THE "FEMME FACTOR" IN ENTREPRENEURSHIP AND THE SETUP OF AN ENVIRONMENT FOR MENTAL HEALTH CONCERNS.

The *Sixth Annual State of Women Owned Business Report*, commissioned by American Express OPEN, found that more than a thousand women-owned businesses are formed each day. They also reported that women-owned firms are employing nearly nine million people.[13]

According to the National Women's Business Council, there are ALSO over nine million women-owned businesses in the United States alone.[14] Despite this, women continue to lack access to some of the most crucial assets, capital, and markets necessary to launch and grow their businesses. When not having access to the same resources for success as our male counterparts, we typically make do with whatever means are available. But imagine knowing full well that, despite owning businesses driving economic growth and bringing money back into the local community, we have access to a mere 2.7 percent of all total venture capital funding.[15]

Not only do women get the short end of the financial stick, but also – depending on the industry – they may have to deal with discrimination through first-hand experiences or second-hand narratives. Take, for example, not being on an equal footing with male colleagues: while you may have aspirations to start something unique, you notice that funding is only offered to fields like childcare, beauty, and fashion. Imagine now, the feelings of rejection when you believe that your ideas are just as valid, if not even more innovative than male counterparts'. When asked about the difficulties of being a leader in a primarily male-dominated space, many women I spoke with confirmed that it was indeed "a man's world," as James Brown sang about.[16] In order to even get a foot in the door, many women have to work strategically, much like a game of chess, often sacrificing much of their personal lives in the process.

I had to work twice as hard to get into my position. I had to be the first to arrive, and the last to leave. I battled with feelings of guilt about not being there for my kid the way I wanted while understanding that I had to prove my worth so that I could provide for my family. My colleagues came in late, got into arguments with customers, and didn't always finish their work assignments properly yet nothing ever happened to them, and they'd have no problem letting me know that. Year after year they made the same money as me even though I was given more responsibilities. However, if I made a tiny mistake I'd get chewed out for it. And I would never get an apology once it was found out I wasn't at fault. By the time I was offered a "seat," I felt like I was only given the opportunity because they had to fill it and no one else wanted to do what I was willing and most qualified to do. It was like they asked "Who wants this?" and I'd raise my hand while they kept looking around me to see if somebody, anybody but me would take the lead. When there was a meeting of "heads," the woman who hired me started my introduction by rattling off my credentials, and that I came from the north, as if there needed to be an explanation for her choice in me, as if I needed an excuse for my presence in the room. Even now in my current position, I feel like I'm being watched under the scrutiny of a fine-tooth comb. It's very stressful and taking a toll on me. – "Amaya"

Now imagine: since childhood you've always been told in some way, shape, or form to sit in the corner, know your place, and be grateful for whatever life hands you. Perhaps a father figure remarked off-handedly that he didn't like smart women, or a male teacher said math and science were for the big boys, or a woman you admired explained that your goal in life should be to marry, not deflate a man's ego by being too ambitious, and have at least 2.6 well-mannered little children[17] (I'm still trying to figure out how one gets a sixth of a child). What if you are raised to believe that no matter your level of education, or contributions to the economy, a woman's place was best suited in the home caring for others – not because it's intricate and respected work that takes strategic planning, budgeting skills, a ton of patience and flexibility – but because it's considered low-level work for a less superior brain. Such scenarios happen to the best of us, replaying old messages with negative connotations and carrying them into our adulthood. These messages are what I've come to identify as the negative inner voice that often causes women to self-sabotage various areas of their lives, preventing attainment of total wellness and fulfillment.

As women raised in a patriarchal society, we learn that leadership is commonly defined and standardized by men. Therefore, traits associated with male leadership such as dominance, competitiveness, and power are prized and valued in the workplace, while women and their hormones are meant to be left at home. In an effort to not appear weak, women push aside what's a fundamental part of their feminine mystique – such as grace, intuition, fortitude, and coming together to uplift one another in sisterhood as we rise to greater heights. And to "belong" if even on the outskirts, they will shame other women for being too feminine just as much as for being too masculine.

The issue then – and proposed structure for mental health concerns outside of biological reasons – is socialization. In other words, the way young girls have been raised to be women in their society. According to *The Concept of Women,* the social concept of women in the history of western philosophy has been rather demoralizing, as women were perceived as subservient to men.[18] Modern-day society may argue that that viewpoint was the past; however, in the twenty-first century women are still treated as second-class citizens in certain parts of the world. Even today in "First World" countries, women are still a small minority sitting in the coveted "seat at the table."

Why am I dredging this up? Because according to the World Health Organization (WHO): "Gender determines the differential power and control men and women have over the socioeconomic determinants of their mental health and lives, their social position, status and treatment in society and their susceptibility and exposure to specific mental health risks."[19]

Whether calling ourselves "female," "feminine," "lady," or "woman" – in our society, to ignore all of who we are is a surefire way to show up as a leader, yet beating to the drum of somebody else. How can we define success on our own terms if we're driven continually to live under someone's definition of who we should be, and their unrealistic set of expectations and rules?

And because there is such a contradiction of roles we have to play, I am not surprised to have heard so many women say "I've been depressed my whole life," as if it were a pastime in which we all partake and accept as sacrosanct. Even the very first time I went to therapy, my counselor concluded that I too had been fairly depressed my whole life. Why is that? How is it possible that so many of us with a wide range of backgrounds and cultural upbringings – from financially well-off to struggling and living off of cheap ramen noodle packs – fit right in, nice and snug, with the estimated three hundred million people (more often than not women) who suffer from depression?[20]

Is it a chemical imbalance in the brain? Is it just a symptom rather than an ailment or disease itself? Is it a societal issue? Is it an epidemic? There's so many different revelations from multiple sources. Perhaps it's a potpourri-like blend of all.

But if you ask people who are experiencing an episode of depression, or are triggered to the point that they can't seem to get out of the bed, none of that matters! What we do know is how depression feels as we experience it. What we do know is that depression is often coupled with another mental health concern we have come to know as anxiety. And what we know is that according to the National Alliance on Mental Illness (NAMI) 90 percent of people who die by suicide have clinical depression or another diagnosable mental disorder.[21] So instead of arguing over semantics, here is what our peers have to say about experiencing mental illness.

It can be a blessing and a curse in some ways. Sometimes I can start obsessing and really get things done, but in some ways, it holds me back because I'm always nervous about messing up. That's when you start missing deadlines and hiding under the guise of work, with business you can have a meltdown and nobody will notice it, you can easily isolate and hide your pain. At work, I can put on a mask. – "Eleanor"

I've always struggled with anxiety, but when I was diagnosed with post-partum, I questioned if I was less than because of it. It was more than a label more like a sentence that said "something is wrong with you-something is bad." – "Jane"

I would sit in a corner and fold myself into an upward sitting fetal like position and just stare off at the 4 walls surrounding me. Sometimes I'd cry, other times I wanted to scream, sometimes I just hurt so bad that the tears stopped falling and I no longer had a voice to let out the anguish I held deep inside. I wanted to remove myself from myself for a brief nanosecond of relief! Yet I just sat and stared at nothing for hours feeling paralyzed wondering if maybe my existence was all just a really bad dream. – "Tia"

I used to think I was just burnt out. But I realized burn out is mere exhaustion. Depression feels like "what am I here for anymore?" – "Willow"

ANXIETY AND DEPRESSION AND ENTREPRENEURIAL MELTDOWNS ... OH MY!

This book primarily focuses on the psycho-social aspects of mental health problems rather than the bio-psycho. However, the women I interviewed all reported different mental health concerns, some tied to chronic ailments of the body. For example, some reported: being diagnosed with a bipolar disorder by a psychiatrist or with depression by a family doctor; having a history of addiction; a family history of mental disorders; and additional health issues and physical disabilities that contributed to their mental disorders. Because of that, I don't want to dismiss or make light of the mind-body connection. Women who have endocrine related problems such as thyroid issues and hormonal imbalance, or other related matters such as PMS (premenstrual syndrome) and endometriosis also have an increased risk for certain mental health disorders.[22] Alisa Vitti's *Woman Code* dives much deeper into the mind-body connection for women's health concerns.[23] The blog of Kelly Brogan, M.D., a holistic women's health psychiatrist, may also be worth a read.

I do, however, want to focus on commonalities shared. All of the women I interviewed reported struggling with anxiety, and/or having emotional meltdowns associated with running a business. There was also a strong correlation between my investigation participants and the mental disorder of depression, specifically.

Before proceeding, I wanted to get (and provide) some clarity about the two most prevalently reported disorders (depression and anxiety), and reached out to colleague and mentor, Angela Clack, Psy.D, of Clack Associates, LLC. She explained that "simply put, depression has different looks for different people. For some it's a pervasive sadness, for some debilitating features show. They may eat too much or not enough, sleep too much or not enough. They may have feelings of hopelessness, and a loss of sense of self. As for anxiety, it looks like a situation in which you cannot control —and you're struggling with – the fact that you can't control it."

Here are a few stories that summarized what the majority of the women reported about anxiety and depression, and how these specific conditions impacted running their businesses.

I was recently diagnosed bipolar, but I have a long history of being treated for clinical depression with talk therapy and medication. In the beginning, I was always so tired and I'd procrastinate a lot. At one point in my life, I ended up going bankrupt. But I had a family to provide for so I began to do what I could to make money which was cleaning. When I got back on my feet I learned from experience that I had to build passive income streams and subcontract for the times when I go through those down periods so I'd still have revenue coming in. – "Eleanor"

As a business owner, when I'm depressed I don't feel like doing anything. I feel really insignificant. But my depression didn't always show up outwardly; in public, I'd be like Dr. Jekyll and Mr. Hyde. It was easier to do things already in place like client work, but it was a challenge to do the things that needed to get done for growth. I disappear on Facebook and don't show up to market my business. — "Tia"

When I have anxiety, I overanalyze situations; I have deep feelings of inadequacy. I'm nervous about not finishing anything I start. I'm convinced that I'll mess something up. — "Amaya"

When I'm struggling with anxiety, I want to be involved in a lot of things but I'm very apprehensive, and unsure of myself to step more fully into anything else at the time. I'm scared I may have another major depressive episode. So, I bury myself in work. I hide my fears away by making myself useful through my businesses. — "Willow"

I'm still able to do work for my clients because it's natural; in a way it's a distraction, and I have a team in place. The problem is when I'm asked to do anything more than that. Apathy gets in the way of success. I get complacent because someone else will carry my workload for me. When I'm depressed, sharing my insights, chiming in on strategy … I don't want to do that. — "Jane"

In *Business from Bed,* author and coach Joan Friedlander wrote that "when a major life event, [such as a mental illness diagnosis] changes you, a line has been drawn in the sand. There is a life as you knew it before, and life as it is now… It is likely to be one of the most challenging journeys of your lifetime, one that requires you to garner strength you never knew you had, while pulling into the deep shadows of the greatest fears you have ever known." She then goes on to say that "it helps to understand the nature of the journey and what threatens your revival."[24] I agree. At this point, it is my belief that most entrepreneurs experience some anxious thoughts while running a business. Because of that, entrepreneurs have to be mindful of their health and wellness in general. I believe, however, that when you also struggle with a diagnosed mental disorder, you have to take extra care to be prepared in all possible ways. You have to become super aware of your triggers, and what happens to you once fully triggered. You have to be cognizant of changes in your temperament when you take your medications, and how your body reacts to the meds so you can adjust working hours accordingly (i.e. to your body's rhythm). The point is to accept and acknowledge that while your diagnosis doesn't define you, it is not something to ignore – especially as it relates to handling business and making a living.

What I found most interesting is that these women *willed* themselves to come to a place of acceptance in order to seek help. That may not have been the case in all instances, but honestly, it is far too easy to pretend mental illness is "all in our heads."

The denial and unnamed emotions.

It's natural to want to feel that your life is under control. It's easier to press on and wear a smile like a mask, pretending everything is A-OK as you perform for the audience you've concocted in your mind, i.e. co-workers/colleagues, relatives, friends, employees, contractors, etc. Because as women we have to either be somewhat weak and docile, or strong enough to be seen as equal to a man. However, we are (obviously) not male, and there are men influencing others who like to point that out, and often, in the struggle for dominance and power. But both sides lose this argument when it comes to mental illness or mental health "disruptions" of any kind – "something" seen as ultimate weakness. "Something" that is avoided for fear of a diagnoses, and if diagnosed, then denied for fear of stigma and an admittance of defeat.

The truth is we suffer lots of mini-traumatic experiences that (of course) cause emotional response we have to sit comfortably uncomfortably through, like anger, disappointment, and yes, even "the blahs." But as these emotions build up, we try to bury them deep in the crevices of our soul hiding our humanity behind *what we think we should be* ... and *how we think we should act* ... despite the unnamed feelings experienced, yet denied.

So, we "one glass of wine" a night the feelings away, or sleep or work overtime, or buy things we don't need to "retail therapy" them away. We tell our support system that we aren't the problem ... they are! We say that we can't afford or don't have time to seek help, or that our family and friends – who aren't trained in anything other than being a family member or friend – are all the help needed. We learn we can just pray or live with it because everyone from the "good old days" had the same issues, yet didn't complain or have as many "mind sicknesses." When running a business, however, ignoring mental health issues invites varying degrees of sabotage into the work atmosphere, whether we are cognizant of the dangers or not.

Dear Mental Health Disorder, you and I, we have unfinished business.

Because I've worked online for a number of years, I was able to "see" (via social media) the constant written documentation of the frustrations that arise from starting and running a business. I'm witness to the excitement of a new entrepreneurial launch, the sense of accomplishment obvious within a post about an *Inc.* article citing the business owner as a source expert. I also read about the anger and frustration of women being overlooked by a male investor for a male competitor when their product is just as good and viable – if not better. I've seen small business owners happily share pictures of the lunch specials one day, and a few days later read personal social media posts that they're so very tired, and with a heavy heart will have to close down their precious dream café. I've seen people giddily blog about quitting a job just like their hero lifestyle entrepreneur so they can work on a beach while sipping piña coladas and even make money in their sleep. Later, that once-enthusiastic individual later blogs about how much they paid to said hero entrepreneur for continued freedom from a traditional corporate office, while they then had to go back to a job because of all the debt incurred trying to emulate "Mike" and his entrepreneurial lifestyle.

I began to think there must be a revolving door, on one side representing success and the other failure. But over time I've learned even that isn't a very accurate description. On either side, you can experience the other. You can have great financial success, but be at war with yourself. You could experience failure, but see how losing an exasperating client was the best thing that could happen. Failure is not always a negative, in my humble opinion. It is just as much a part of the human experience as aging and grief. However, defeat – that voice that echoes in words and phrases such as: "I just can't stand to live with myself anymore" – is what calls my attention. The reasons why someone would think *that* is what concerns me.

Here's the thing about the business world. We literally have to fight against our reactions to often unsolicited advice about our standing as "successful" business professionals. Sure, some amazing bloggers write that we are more than the success of our business – and I couldn't agree more. However, when stepping out of that sacred place where you get to love on yourself, you have to go into a world full of people who do *not* have sacred spaces for the same purpose. As a result, such individuals don't see the truth and beauty of who you are, which translates into valuing you for, first and foremost, what you can do to make their lives easier and less painful; and, second, for what people who have influence have to say about you.

So, we chase the money. Taking it further, as the song by The Lox goes, we chase *Money, Power & Respect.*[25] And as the alpha at the top, you are greeted by tons of faux friendliness and adoring and respectful fans who sing your praises (especially if you offer them an affiliate commission). But for the woman who rose above the ashes not for money, not for the power, and not for the kind of respect that is born of fear from repercussions and fiery wrath – reaching a point where being known, appreciated, supported, liked and *really seen for who she is beyond her brand* ... that possibility is questionable at best. Who is really *for her* and who is only *for what she can do*? These quick passing thoughts and questions of worth and value (the kind not measured with a price tag regardless of how much money is sitting in your bank account), can do some serious damage in time. "It's lonely at the top" is an understatement when statistics indicate that one in ten Americans according to the National Center of Health Statistics are on anti-depressant pills.[26] With all this social media to connect us globally and advances in technology to make us more efficient for the powers that be, there seems to be a major virus in the matrix.

CHAPTER 2

Why Entrepreneurship Feels Like the Most Viable Option

———

*If I didn't define myself for myself, I would be crunched
into other people's fantasies for me and eaten alive.*

—Audre Lorde, *Sister Outsider: Essays & Speeches*, 2007

"What do you want to be when you grow up?" I am going to guess
that everyone reading was presented with some version of that question during their lifetime. I don't remember exactly what my answer
was originally, but I know that after some socialization, after seeing
what I saw and feeling what I felt, I knew from very early on that I
wanted to help people. The field of psychology was fascinating and
I wanted to become a counselor. When I was younger my grandmother's insurance broker, a man from west Africa, once asked me
that question. I shared my desire to be a counselor; he then proceeded
to tell me I should become a doctor. That a doctor would be better for
my family and I'd be much happier. He then asked me to chant "I am
going to be a doctor" multiple times and I dutifully replied … later, I
compromised with his logic and decided to become a psychiatrist. By
the time I got to high school and just about failed every class in the

math and science curriculum, I concluded medicine in any form was simply not for me. However, I really loved science and I still wanted to help children who came from dysfunctional families and so circled back to the idea of being a counselor, and informed my high school guidance counselor. There are horror stories about guidance counselors discouraging students whom, through conscious or unconscious biases, they deemed as "less than." But I was lucky – my own guidance counselor stuck with me when I promised to get my grades up in order to go to a university. I had decided that once in college, I would first tackle classes representing my weakest areas; obtain the assistance of a tutor if needed; and then take a bunch of courses in which I could excel. That, in turn, would bring my GPA back up so I could get into a good graduate school.

My plan worked! I improved so much I got a scholarship created specifically for students who made miraculous comebacks by their junior and senior years (I guess I wasn't alone in my struggles if such scholarships exist). By my final year of college and with special permission, I overloaded my classes beyond the normal amount, started a job in the field I loved, got engaged, and graduated university with high honors. (Later I will delve deeper into the elements necessary to make this amazing change, because while unique, my story in its essence is not uncommon.)

Because I was from a working-class family and had more interest in being rescued by my prince charming and making money right then and there, I got married before the ink on my degree dried and took the first counseling job that would hire someone with only a bachelor's degree – a social services position in a girls' group home. During this time, I held on to the dream that one day I'd create my own youth center for girls just like me.

Fast forward to a divorce and many lost dreams later: I burned out while working in the substance abuse field, and had no clue what to do now that I was a grown up with no job and a mortgage to pay.

While I had no interest in being a business owner at that time, I was pushed into entrepreneurship. My mother was a local government administrator, but a single mom with four kids (hence the "working class" reference). I honestly have no idea what my father did, but my uncle – the closest I had to a male role model – was a veteran who also worked for the government. Essentially, the influencers in my life were all hard-working people who believed in seeking out and working "good and stable" jobs to take care of their families; taking an occasional vacation or two throughout their career; surviving the cold, harsh world; and eventually retiring. Under this mindset I was to go to college, get a good job, get married, have a family, and live happily-ever-after … the end. But then, of course, life happened … as it does for so many.

BUSINESS, BECAUSE THE OTHER OPTIONS LOOK DIRE.

I did it because there were no other options. I wasn't able to work due to the circumstances of leaving an abusive marriage, being homeless at one point, and caring for my children with disabilities. I needed to rebuild my life, so I launched my company. – K.T.

My physical aliment led to work discrimination, and layoffs. I felt like society said "we don't want you around," so after years of looking for a job I started my own business. – A.T.

In *Business from Bed,* Friedlander wrote about being let go the day after returning from a disability leave. Even though it was unplanned, self-employment was attractive to her after she became very ill. She would now have control over her physical environment by setting her schedule around personal needs such as doctors' appointments. She would also be able to do work that mattered and was meaningful to her and those with whom she worked.[27]

I too was let go from my job a day or two after returning from a disability leave. Before that I thought long and hard about what I really wanted to do with my life, and concluded my job wasn't it; apparently my employers were on the same page.

We all have unique background stories about moving from one set path in the past to another in the present. Some like us are very much "toilet paper entrepreneurs," using those last three sheets of manufactured tree and making the most with what we're given.[28] For others, the road toward entrepreneurship has already been paved, or at least something that was always on the horizon.

BUSINESS, BECAUSE IT WAS A CHOICE.

On the other side of the spectrum are women I've interviewed and met along my business journey who deliberately chose this path, and made plans to pursue it from the door.

> *I could never see myself doing a job. People make me edgy and anxious. I prefer to interact with people on my own terms where I can control my anxiety. — B.A.*

> *My parents were entrepreneurial and taught me to be as well. Before my current business, I owned a traditional brick and mortar. — D.C.*

My job was really stressful. I had a friend come to me and tell me about a business opportunity where I could work from home. I quit my job to pursue it. – T.S.

Of course, there are also those of us who chose to put one foot in two doors at the same time. And such individuals become side-hustle queens who without a doubt often have to play the balancing act.

Finally, there are also women who embrace business through their world-famous fathers and/or mothers; or parents who freelanced on the side and encouraged their daughters to always have some sort of hustle going in addition to a regular source of income. Some were entitled to an inheritance in the form of a family-owned business.

If they ask "why," "why" tell them…

I also felt exploring the underlying intentions for entering the realm of entrepreneurship to be worthwhile. Because it is so very easy to end up disenchanted, disillusioned, disgruntled – and consequently finding ourselves wanting to disassociate from our businesses – I believe that possessing a deeply meaningful "why," empowers us to become resilient in order to fight for the reason behind what we do. With this in mind, I asked women if there was a subconscious reason for their entrepreneurship beyond "I was laid off from my job" or "I inherited my father's business."

TEDx speaker Simon Sinek came to be known for the concept of starting with your "why"/ purpose when starting a business, rather than the "what" or even the "how." In his book *Start With Why*, Sinek writes, "Without why, any attempt at authenticity will almost always be inauthentic… After you have clarity of why, are you disciplined and accountable to your own values and guiding principles and are consistent in all you say and do."[29]

Keeping Sinek's concepts top-of-mind, I posed the following questions to women entrepreneurs in targeted social media forums:

- "When you first started your business, did you know your 'why' or did it come to you later along your business journey?"
- "What sparked your why?"
- "Did your 'why' change up over time?"

These are some of the responses I received:

I've always wanted to help others financially and emotionally and needed the creative freedom to do so. – M.L.

My daughter [sparked my "why"]. She has special needs that required specific care. I needed a schedule that would cater to her needs. She was diagnosed on Thursday; I gave notice that I was quitting my job on Friday. – J.T.

I come from a very blue-collar family; we really struggled financially growing up and never talked about money. But then I went to an "elite" college and started working on Wall Street immediately after. I very quickly realized that the wealthy have access to significantly more, higher-quality resources that help them make smart, successful investment decisions. I had to confront a moral dilemma – that my job was to basically make rich people even richer. That's what I was "getting out of bed for" every day. Meanwhile people like my friends and family were struggling to even understand their 401(k)s. I started my company to teach people about investing and provide hedge-fund quality resources to the masses. – T. N.

When I first started out, I did what I did to help families like my own. Eventually, I felt called to do more. My reason for doing what I did evolved, it grew for the bigger role I had to play.
– S.S.

Regardless, the path toward entrepreneurship, the common characteristics of women who appear on Forbes "most powerful" lists has been a topic of study for quite some time – apparently so we can emulate their success. Taking that line of thought a step further, we might even have certain traits in common that make the path of business ownership appealing to begin with. Barry Moltz, a small business/entrepreneurship author and speaker, wrote a book entitled *You Need to Be A Little Crazy* to express what many of us suspected: pursuing entrepreneurship is a bit unconventional.[30]

In *Are Entrepreneurs "Touched with Fire?"*, Dr. Freeman's research also concluded that not only are business owners prone to having mental health concerns (sometimes simply due to the weight of responsibility in shouldering other people's livelihood), but also people with certain mental health concerns tend toward pursuing entrepreneurship.[31] Apparently, it takes a little "fire" to even want to be entrepreneurs and run businesses!

Setting this viewpoint aside, throughout my time researching various aspects of women leaders – including what motivated women entrepreneurs to continue on a path fraught with so much uncertainty – I noticed certain undeniable, shared commonalities. One was similar business values, the most common of which was a sense of freedom. I'll dig more into the significance of this particular value later on.

But because of the correlation between mental health conditions and entrepreneurship, perhaps it is not so surprising that many who are truly called to the path entrepreneurship feel virtually unemploy-able – mostly because we're round pegs who are not interested in fit-ting into any square holes. We may even claim our issues, but will not go further. Meaning, we will not explore matters or will simply deem them secondary to making money and so inadvertently start our own business in order to create an environment that feels "safe," that en-ables us to hide behind our productivity and outward achievements. That is, until we can't hide our burdens any more.

ENTREPRENEURSHIP, IT REVS ME UP. ENTREPRENEURSHIP, IT TEARS ME DOWN.

There seemed to be two sides of the same coin when talking about how mental health conditions affected business. On one side, mental illness was a catalyst for change; a warning signal that something was amiss and to turn around before you crash. On the other side, mental illness looked much the same; however, its appearance occurred after you left the dock to discover a new land and claim your place in the world. The boats were burned and you're left losing the battle and seeing nothing but defeat. Let's end this chapter with a brief overview of the positive effects of mental disorders, and then really dig into the perception of a hopeless battle in Chapter 3.

Throughout my writing process, many women who knew I was working on this book sent me anything and everything related to this topic to aid my research. As a result, I got to read quite a few articles from major publications such as *Inc.* and *Forbes*, and personal blogs from entrepreneurs who found their way to success on their own terms. Articles that proudly boasted about an entrepreneur who fought through depression and built multimillion dollar businesses, commentaries that talked about battling depression while running a business. The most encouraging news of all the articles was found in the aforementioned clinical research conducted by Dr. Freeman, which found that despite mental health disorders it was indeed quite possible to be a successful entrepreneur. Not only was it possible, but with the right resources to nurture the quirks that came along with mental illness, we could actually leverage certain traits that seemed to be prevalent in those with mental health disorders so that more entrepreneurs could experience greater business success.[32]

But for every great success story, I couldn't help but to wonder how many women thought of mental health disorders as something you simply overcame. I worried for those who "made it," and wondered if they operated from a place that left no room to keep their mental health in a system of checks and balances. Or did they throw caution to the wind, deciding that mental illness was no longer their truth; no longer a part of who they were and therefore no longer something to dwell on; no longer something to keep under consideration … even as it relates to fellow entrepreneurs who may be still in the struggle.

I know admitting to mental health issues is uncomfortable, but going even further and advocating on behalf of a past experience … yikes! And so, in the movement of "positive thinking creates positive reality" we oftentimes bury thoughts that occur when we're triggered, hoping to drown out inner voices of resistance with more goal setting, and getting more done.

We know what life looked like before we dove (or were pushed) to our career of choice. While the mirage of stability looks appetizing, and the lure of falling in line and letting someone else lead the pack sings to us when we're exhausted from our journeys, we know we can't go backwards. We must press on. We press on toward the prize to which we have been called, toward our version of success.

CHAPTER 3

The Pursuit of Success (What an Epic and Draining Journey!)

———

*For everything in this journey of life we are on, there is
a right wing and a left wing: for the wing of love there is
anger; for the wing of destiny there is fear; for the wing of
pain there is healing… There is a generation of people who
idealize perfection as the existence of only one of these wings
every time. But I see that a bird with one wing is imperfect.
An angel with one wing is imperfect. A butterfly with one
wing is dead. So this generation of people strive to always cut
off the other wing in the hopes of embodying their ideal of
perfection, and in doing so, have created a crippled race.*

– C. JOYBELL C., "C. JOYBELL C. QUOTES," GOODREADS (N.D.)

IN THE LAST CHAPTER, I briefly mentioned the value of freedom,
which many of my interviewees shared. In this chapter, I want to talk
about how this value ties into a woman's definition of success. Here's
how some of my interview participants defined success:

There's different levels of success for different stages of your life. At one point in my life, climbing the corporate ladder was my version of success. After becoming a mom, my priorities changed, success then became doing what I loved and being able to be there for my children. – "Eleanor"

Success is having the financial freedom to do what I want so I can make an impact in the world and actually see that impact. – "Amaya"

Success is feeling fulfilled while doing work I love, and being healthy financially, and emotionally in order to give back. – "Jane"

Success is helping other women find their success and having the freedom and flexibility to do it in a way that makes me happy. – "Tia"

Success is freedom, independence, and the ability to have choices. – "Willow"

Freedom, there's nothing like it! To be free in a world that does it best to stifle your most authentic self by trying to conform you to societal norms – this is the work of a lifetime and most definitely a great accomplishment. It is no surprise that the thought of striking out and building up a business on your own, or simply the concept of *owning*, presents an opportunity for freedom. There's a reason get-rich-quick schemes still exist and people keep falling for them. But what if freedom was an ultimate goal, while owning and the responsibilities that ownership brings felt like suffocation … stifling the very freedom we craved? What if the work involved to acquire our freedom made us feel unhappy?

THE OVER-SATURATION OF HAPPINESS.
There are a lot of researchers, hobby investigators, and knowledge seekers looking to understand happiness, and how to get more of it. Long before the movie *The Pursuit of Happyness*[33] came out, seeking the answer to the age-old question: "How can I experience lasting happiness?" was an enchanting siren many would not resist. Culturally, when we began showcasing "happily ever after" in media and books, the thought of bad feelings and suffering was unwelcomed, even chastised away. When we don't like the world as is, we seek out new worlds, looking for Utopia, even at the cost of dispelling anyone who previously found Utopia (as we define it) and the resources it possesses. The collision of different worldviews with regard to what happiness should look like creates a schism: first with each other; and then within ourselves to justify the means of obtaining our very own "happily ever after."

Within each individual mind there is a battlefield of opposing views and an internal struggle warring to win out for the truth. Is the happiness we seek how we would define it? Or was this particular definition of happiness implanted in our subconscious through our social up-rearing? By whose standards do we truly work and live?

Now, reading what you just read, was it triggering? Did bringing up the historical facts about creating happiness at the expense of others' lives and well-being make you feel like you needed to defend your position? If not, I promise you it has for others. I've seen it countless times in support groups and online forums, especially when politics and religion are involved. But if we are to pursue taking a deeper look at why we are obsessed with success and the feelings of elation we believe accomplishment will bring, I think we owe it to ourselves to see how this objective translates on a larger societal level, in order to reveal the shadow that lurks in the mists. It is by looking at the entire picture, not just the nice and pretty things, and stepping out from the confines of our cocoons, that we are able to fully experience a joy that lasts.

> *I get quiet so I can process my emotions. When I get triggered, I let myself feel and go through pain so I can find out why. Why am I feeling triggered, what's really happening? I want to be able to say that despite the uncomfortable that I feel, I still have joy. — "Amaya"*

Not everyone is willing to do this when they become triggered, however, and one reason is because we resist getting still and quiet. We resist painful feelings. When we look at media outlets and peers, all we see is winners and their happy smiling faces celebrating yet another milestone victory. We then feel we have to step up in order to keep up even if we are at odds with ourselves in the process.

Socialized to compare ourselves to an idealized image.

Michael Gerber published a book called *The E-Myth Revisited,* which stated that it was a "myth that most people who start small businesses are entrepreneurs." And that there was a "fatal assumption that an individual who understands the technical work of a business can successfully run a business that does that technical work."[34] Even though this book was targeted specifically to the small business market, I believe that business owners of any size find themselves having to make tough choices when feeling the pressures that come from business dealings. Out of tough choices emerge personal inquisitions. Comparing ourselves to one another and battling "imposter syndrome" when we believe we don't measure up is not uncommon in women and likely to show up in such circumstances.

Mental health issues tell you you're not good enough, but taking it a step further — that something is inherently wrong with you. — "Eleanor"

You downplay your abilities in what you're actually capable of. You doubt yourself a lot. You don't want to be around people because you feel like you don't belong. — "Tia"

When considering my own self-assigned role of business owner, I would question myself: "Do I go back to where was I was and what I knew, or do I forge ahead into the abyss of the unknown and pursue this pathway that I hope will lead to my definition of success, which encompassed a value of freedom?" In my line of questioning, I wondered if I had what it took to build fortitude and withstand the tests of time. And I often wondered about how bad I wanted to cross this proverbial finish line of success, and if I was mentally fit enough to even run the race. Likewise, women I interviewed would, from time to time, find themselves entering a place of reckless abandon where they questioned the worth of continuing along that particular business path. They also felt downtrodden when questioning whether or not they were mentally fit enough anymore.

Because of the nature of my work, I have the opportunity to talk to women from around the world as a part of business networking. Every once in a while, I even get to step into a "I've been there" role. A colleague introduced me to a young lady just beginning her journey as a new entrepreneur, and I provided my contact information with permission to call. One day she did so and told me about feeling stuck in a rut, unsure of her next steps toward building a business but not being able to let go of the "stability" of a job. We then talked about how it was so rare to hear of people staying at the same job for twenty years or more. I asked if she could have that type of stability, would she want it? She replied that she didn't have it in her to stay in one place for long without getting bored.

Still stuck in a planning and preparation mode, she was unable to truly take off with her business, even with all our talks. It seemed she couldn't focus on moving from the desire to start a business to goal setting and goal accomplishing (a situation further complicated when the business coach she did hire decided to drop all of her clients). The young aspiring entrepreneur felt like she needed someone there to tell her what to do, but at the same time also needed to be her own boss. So, I asked her why. Why did she need to be her own boss? She concluded that they idea of having to be stationed in one place, all day long, essentially felt like a prison sentence.

Success at the start is then about escaping the confines of an oppressive work environment. But without some type of positive reinforcement in that freedom, a suitable replacement for guidance, we often find ourselves suck in the muck. According to social psychologist Eric Fromm, it is a fear of freedom that triggers so many people to the point of paralysis and then finally desperation.[35] Which leaves me to question, just what kind of success are we chasing if fueled by feelings of hopelessness and desperation?

THESE "BLUES" ARE MORE THAN A GOOD SONG LYRIC.
One of the many terms I came across while writing this book was what a good friend and colleague of mine (not so affectionately) called the "entrepreneurial woes." Usually this state of mind started with a conversation about how hard we were working, how tired we were, how we invested every single penny we earned from our business back into our business – and wondering what was "wrong" with us that we did not see any true return on our investments. The investment

wasn't just financial, it was emotional, spiritual, and psychological. We knew this. We also knew we weren't the only ones having the type of conversations we had about our woes. We later dubbed our feelings "entrepreneurial meltdowns" simply because we were left with the ultimate feeling of frustration, anger, and immense sadness which would eventually transform into numbness, and days sprinkled with a dash of malaise that made us want to give up.

> *It looks like my business is doing very well. However, behind the scenes this is not easy. Not only is it not easy, it's crazy. I'm convinced only the crazy become entrepreneurs. You have to be obsessed. I have days when I want to quit five times. I have days when I don't want to get out of bed. I have days when I cry because I'm too tired to work. I have days when I'm cranky and impatient because everyone wants to talk to me. It is just me. I do not have a partner, a branding person, operations person, an assistant, a PR rep, an agent, or a marketing person. I'm working on limited resources and ALL my life savings. I had to learn a lot of skills I didn't know. I stopped shopping. I stopped hanging out. I stopped traveling. I stopped going out to eat. I left a lot of things that made me feel good in the past. I work a lot, rest when I need to... – P.B.*

Yet many times after our meltdowns, I thought about what is known in most 12-step communities as the *Serenity Prayer*, most specifically the line that read "the courage to change the things I can."[36] There were certain external factors we simply had no control over, but what about what was going on deep inside? Could that be changed? I began to question simple concepts that we make so complicated such as self-esteem, self-worth, self-care, and wondering if "love was truly all we need." I took this line of thought a step further and began to wonder if some women who literally had to fight to just see themselves beyond the "other," – did such individuals feel they struggled more than any other to see a return on their business investment?

Even though my own preconceived notions assumed I'd report that women with mental health issues had a "failure to sail" syndrome, that wasn't really the case – at least not among the women I interviewed. Neither depression nor anxiety kept women from leading innovative companies, making multiple six figures, or building a business from which they made a living and obtained the freedom and flexibility they desired. However, entrepreneurial woes/emotional meltdowns and their causes were prevalent enough to warrant taking a closer look.

CONQUER OR BE CONQUERED.

The first time I heard the phrase "burning the boats" and actually paid attention was after listening to a webinar hosted by marketing strategist Amy Porterfield. As most webinars go, you need to tell your audience who you are, what makes you awesome, and why you're the right person to help them be awesome too. Porterfield was telling her story about leaving the employ of Tony Robins (yes, *the* Tony Robins, personal development "guru") and his words of encouragement with a godspeed blessing.[37] And Amy went on to launch a financially successful business as a social media rainmaker, living happily-ever-after, the end ... but of course, rarely if ever does the story go so swimmingly in entrepreneurship. The narrative didn't look that way for Amy as she tells it, and it sure didn't look that way for me and most of the women I've been interviewing over the years.

Therefore, we burn the boats of "normalcy" and do this crazy entrepreneurship thing. We are all fired up, we likely have this awesome business plan written out by a business consultant who knows what they're doing and the sales projections look challenging but definitely obtainable. We spent a good amount on developing excellent branding and marketing and setting up the launch, and then we encounter one problem … crickets. Our picturesque dream of world domination cracks when we begin to perceive our losing battles as the ultimate defeat. Sadly, that perception of loss and failure is the catalyst for a real war, fought on the battlefield of our minds.

Our minds receive so many conflicting messages about who we "should" be that when we fall short of our "should," we either sink or swim toward whatever possibility awaits us. While it is blatantly clear that huge disparities exist between women and men – who gets to run large corporations, for instance – we are given the go-ahead to yell out about our strength and competency. There's the American World War II "We Can Do It!" poster of a woman in blue workers' overalls and red bandana, flexing her muscles and proving to men she has what it takes to make huge strides in the workplace, and hang just like the boys. (The image, however, was originally meant to encourage already hardworking women to work even harder during wartime.)[38] Consequently, women who advance in the workplace are encouraged to work in the same context as their male counterparts, meeting the demands of the same relentless and unrealistic "shoulds" – and for less pay.

We should get a degree, we should hire a business coach, we should eat these foods because that's what this successful person does each day, and even though we should work up to men's standards we should still be very feminine so it appeases the eyes and attracts our male counterparts. Because heaven forbid we don't meet the "should requirements" for having happy, well-adjusted kids and living in the right neighborhoods, having the right relationships with the right school board and soccer moms, because ultimately, we should be perfect.

Truly, perfection is what's required, or the next best thing … which is to only have issues that don't influence the status quo (just being an "other" will trigger peoples' sensibilities, of course). For example, the "issue" of pregnancy is a justifiable reason to pay women less because it's such a huge expense to business. But the "issue" of alcohol abuse, which is more prevalent in men, and a huge expense by way of medical costs and work performance losses in business, is tolerated and too many times covered up.

The point is, if we pay attention to what's being marketed to us on a daily basis not only through media, but also by those who continue to project their own insecurities onto each other in order to save face, we will find an entire mainstream culture of somewhat desperate attempts to attain the virtually unattainable. It is counterculture to resist. Writer and activist Audre Lorde said, "Caring for myself is not self-indulgence, it is self-preservation, and that is an act of political warfare."[39] Therefore, living a "wholehearted" life – as researcher Brené Brown, Ph.D., writes and teaches about[40] – is countercultural. When you're trying to prove your worth in gold (literally), counterculture in any form is seen as career suicide. So, on and on we struggle with temporary euphoric moments fueled by pain and pressure to conform, to be the product. And if we're "successful," we become the producer of a system that imposes the perfectionism trap until we, and those we lead, finally crash and burn.

While struggling to stay afloat, we refuse to show any sign of weakness. This is why I'm not a fan of the phrase "fake it 'til you make it." Perhaps I'm taking the saying out of context, but my theory is many people are also (i.e. taking it out of context) if they make this their mantra when starting a business, or trying to take a business to the revered next-level.

"Fake it 'til you make it" becomes more dangerous to someone with mental and/or emotional health issues. Because our minds are so very vulnerable – perhaps more vulnerable than most – we have to be very careful with the messages allowed to replay in our heads, or we start to believe those ideas to the point of self-destruction.

If people pressure you into thinking no one will support you because they do not want to deal with the issues going on in your mind – this is simply a way of implying that the problem is one you've created and brought upon yourself. Naturally, you will want to disguise the easy-to-pick-up outward expressions (i.e. symptoms) of said issues. By popping a pill that treats the symptoms, we can carry on with our existence faking normal ... however normal is perceived in any given situation. Survival and fitting in go hand-in-hand with the concept of faking it. Accordingly, we press on and try to fit in, seeking approval. We hope that one day when we get what we came here for, we will then go back and right our wrongs; expose our truths; and come out and have real talk with people – because by then we won't care anymore, we will have made our money, and achieved our success.

The problem is when you are standing on a chair, it is so much easier to be pulled down than to bring people up. And once pulled down, before long you forget about standing on a higher level, as well as all about the chair itself. That chair represents purpose, meaning, your "why." When losing touch with and never tapping into your intentions, when simply "faking it" becomes so real that it's no longer an act, you are on your way to spinning out of control.

In this sense of helplessness is when fear creeps in and takes over. Fear-based decisions and the subsequent related behaviors birth emotions such as unease, discomfort, and eventually unworthiness – which then produces opportunities for the seeds of shame to be cultivated, nurtured, and reproduced. In an effort to succeed and to not have to face the feelings experienced from our perceived failures, we do what we think we must in order to preserve our "self." A "self" born out of a need to continue living up to a perception we ourselves created. This false "self" – which may or may not be conventionally successful – leaves us exhausted, frustrated, afraid, and overall mentally unwell.

CHAPTER 4

For Shame and Self-Preservation

*Shame is often referred to as the swampland of the soul
… the swampland of the soul is an important place
to visit, but you would not want to live there.*

*– BRENÉ BROWN, PH.D., THE GIFTS OF IMPERFECTION:
LET GO OF WHO YOU THINK YOU'RE SUPPOSED
TO BE AND EMBRACE WHO YOU ARE, 2010*

MENTAL UNWELLNESS IS AMPLIFIED WITH "stinking" thinking and compulsive behaviors, which produce shame. It is easier to engage in such behaviors when at our core we have fear and a fragile ego to soothe. Fear is a hard concept to grasp if one doesn't correlate the emotion to being threatened on a level of familiarity. Meaning, fear, when unacknowledged, isn't perceived as fear. It is then seen as subjective and open to interpretation. What individuals "should" be afraid of is a judgment call and an open game to "other" people and one's own self. Fear is often confused with other emotions – emotions that make it easier to dismiss, or justify, words and actions. No matter; it doesn't change the fact that fear is a human emotion that leads to anger, hate, reactive behaviors, and shame. When experiencing this range of emotions which can overtake and *become* us, we do not live, work, or lead from an authentic version of ourselves.

> *I have a lot of self-imposed fears: the fear of rejection or the fear of not doing something right. – "Eleanor"*

> *Because of depression and self-limiting beliefs, when I started I had fear of judgement. My first business actually helped me nurture my depression. I hid in it and I played very small. – "Jane"*

> *In some ways, because of these fears we're forced to put on a mask. Social structures uphold this way of being, because of wanting to belong we feel forced to blend in. – "Tia"*

> *Everybody wants to be a "somebody" but the truth is, we already are. Because we don't see that, we seek a stamp of approval. We start comprising our integrity to get that approval, and then we fall by the wayside. Entrepreneurs need to focus on the vision in their soul if we're going to be the best version of ourselves. – "Amaya"*

> *It is lonely at the top. In all that fame and fortune there is a lot of doubt and loneliness. People judge weakness and I fear that kind of judgment. If something wasn't done perfectly I'd second guess myself. It's easy to feel like you're a rag to use and discard when you're struggling to appease people who are only concerned about what you can do for them rather than who you are. – "Willow"*

An academic paper on the role of shame noted that there has been well-documented research that negative emotions are more intensely felt than positive emotions. And of all those negative emotions, shame was the most intensely felt of all. There was also evidence of a link between shame and psychological symptoms, like depression and anxiety.[41]

Despite knowing that there is a correlation between shame and depression and anxiety, we readily perpetuate a cycle of shame. We constantly struggle with feeling disconnected and unworthy, so much so that we lose ourselves in the struggle, trying to people-please our way to acceptance and a false sense of belonging.

FEAR DRIVES A CULTURE OF SHAME.

Why do we embrace a culture of driving ourselves into the ground? When did it become cool to say things like "sleep is for suckers" and "every day I'm hustling"? Why is it acceptable that we grind to the point of insomnia which sparks our "need" for pills to go to sleep, pills to wake up, and caffeine to get going about our day? To what end are we any good as leaders if we aren't around to lead? When reading Christine Arylo's *Madly in Love with Me*, I was blown away by what she had discovered while researching women's thoughts about what self-love represents. Basically, caring about your own well-being was considered selfish and egotistical.[42] Based off of what I've read in numerous studies, and my own observations, it seems both women and men have it embedded into their psyche that women are to be selfless givers and nurturers.

That as women, we are supposed to fulfill our duties to society and take care of ourselves just enough so we can continue giving anything asked of us seems inherently wrong.

The further I look back in the history of mankind, the more it seems that wellbeing is a privilege for the people who win the history wars and get to tell the stories. Health and wealth in every area of one's life was only a given to those who knew how to divide and conquer.

Social stratification has long existed as a system within a society that ranks categories of people into a hierarchy. In sociology, there is a theory that assumes that social structures and processes in society exist because they serve important functions for society's stability and continuity. Theorists who expound this view are called functionalists. In this worldview, some jobs are more important than other jobs and only exceptional people have the ability to acquire skills for the most important jobs; therefore, such individuals should be rewarded as the crème de la crème. The *Hunger Games* books and movies are a concrete example of social stratification systems in popular culture today.[43] Functionalists are correct that systems do indeed function to maintain a stability and continuity, which begs the question: Isn't the foundation of division based on *fear of losing perceived limited resources for survival?* Is it because of that fear that those who perceive a loss of supposed limited resources *shame others into submission?*

Shaming what they don't understand, and hating what they can't conquer.

In a world full of people who are fearful and living in tremendous shame, both as receivers of being shamed and perpetuators of shame, it is inevitable that there are people uncomfortable with even talking about situations they don't understand. If something is outside of their realm of experience, – and even an inkling of fear exists that that said thing could jeopardize their way of being – in order to carry on with their lives, they may box it, give it a label, and keep on moving. Lack of understanding can easily become close-mindedness and an inadvertent expectation of outside leadership to fill in the gap. This tendency for giving up one's power – to follow anyone perceived as more knowledgeable and powerful – opens doors for a small segment of influencers to dictate a "normal" way of behaving toward something, under the guise of group consensus. There have been fearful leaders who understood and therefore campaigned on fear to win over the masses, often resulting in large scale genocides. There have also been leaders who understood and worked to move people through fear and liberate their countries.

In a personal encounter with someone who falls outside the confines of a box given triggers can occur. It has always been my observation that people are triggered when they come upon those with mental health issues. I find that our interactions with one another can be mirrors reflecting truths within our hearts. For some, interacting with illness that is not understood is showing them a self they do not want to see or deal with. It is a mirror held up that tells them to turn away because mommy and/or daddy did not raise them that way. What way? Weak. That mirror of truth shows weakness; where the ego needs to feel strength, perceived weakness of others that triggers the self *becomes a permission slip* – not only to be un-empathetic, but also to be condescending, finger pointing, and discriminating. We will fight tooth and nail to protect ourselves from any representation of that which makes us feel triggered.

I came from an era where you swept things under the rug; we didn't focus on things like self-awareness. – "Eleanor"

In our culture, we are taught to be stoic and "keep it moving." My family enforced this way of being. I would rarely see anyone crying, rarely were we allowed to show emotion. – "Tia"

In the past I self-medicated, I felt like drinking helped keep me sane. I knew I was going down the path of destruction but did it anyway. I didn't want to seek help because it would mean that I was one of "them" and not me. – "Jane"

I had a young lady seek me out for mentorship; she quit her job to be a freelancer but struggled a lot with anxiety because she had no money, and was relying on her boyfriend who wasn't very supportive. She had super negative energy while trying to network and grow her business. It's like she wanted clients but didn't want to remove the barriers hindering her success, so she kept shooting herself in her own foot. – "Amaya"

The Stigma Within

We also can't begin to heal what we won't acknowledge or don't understand. And we most certainly can't begin to heal what we are afraid of dealing with. Unfortunately, mental illness scares the daylights out of people, including those diagnosed in the first place. Witnessing someone during an episode brings about a bevy of emotional responses. When we see, right in front of us, someone acting in any way that does not register as "normal" (to our senses) we react. Sometimes, our reactions reveal our most undisciplined selves. This is because it's easy to act cool, calm, and collected when nothing is upsetting your way of being. However, when under an "attack" outcomes are highly unpredictable. One reason I can personally think of for this response: the attack is unseen. Compared to most common physical health concerns, mental health concerns typically aren't seen as easily by the naked eye. If someone is physically deformed, on crutches, or bandaged up, we can see that. But we can't see what's going on within, nor do we completely understand the human brain. That's why it's easy, very easy, to brush off mental illness as "it's all in her head" – meaning, a made-up disorder; something that is not real.

I've talked to many people with diagnosed mental health disorders, and not one of them told me they happily accepted the finding.

Felt relieved to name something that felt unnamable, acknowledgment perhaps, but not outright acceptance. Taking this point even further, I've learned from listening and reading a lot that using a diagnosis to excuse your life, or lack thereof, isn't an acceptance of fate – no, it's more a concession. I write that hesitantly, because I understand why people have chosen a path of no hope for a life that has set, narrowly-defined parameters for what is considered "normal." This society has been very clear about what kind of "crazy" we can accept: highly functional; and what kind we can't: highly dependent.

The business world is no different. As long as someone with, let's say … Asperger's syndrome can compose the most beautiful songs – songs that make people feel good, songs that bring in money (and lots of it), then that individual is alright, they're contributing. As long as the startup founder who is very clearly … troubled, but in a manic state is coming up with amazing ideas, getting out there, and accomplishing more in a day than most would in their lifetime – it's cool. As long as this individual is being charismatic and making investments soar, it doesn't matter about the sleepless nights, the pills to get through the day, the thoughts of suicide in the middle of bumper to bumper traffic.

We see and know these things; those of us with more "acceptable" issues live these things to a certain extent – yet we ourselves cannot even tolerate what most frightens us. We can't even accept our own distress within. We don't want it. We don't want *to not be* normal. Whatever "normal" is *supposed* to be. So, we do what most people do when in response to a perceived harmful event, attack, or threat to survival. We react.

In other words, we get down with the get down, or we get out of dodge. Sometimes, though, we freeze and become so numb to circumstances that if the situation isn't looking like imminent doom we take life-one day at a time, but without really trying.

> *No, I don't really have a specific routine for ongoing mental health care, when I'm not feeling triggered. – "Willow"*

SELF-SABOTAGE.

There's a common, classic motif in any number of older, subtitled films that I often watch: an old woman hunched over and carrying a heavy load on her back. She slowly shuffles down a dirt road and struggles to get on a bus full of people lost in their own worlds, doing their own things. No one offers her help or a seat – and to be fair, she also didn't ask for help. So, there the woman stands with this huge pack: stacks on tops of stacks of packages, all bundled together. But then a stranger comes onto the bus and offers her help. Usually the old lady fights the good Samaritan, screaming that he's a thief trying to steal her burden, which of course she views as her precious goods.

I'm not sure how or when the perfect package of gifts we're given at the time of our existence becomes a load too heavy to bear alone, but we willingly carry what we didn't start our journey with – and we're seemingly expected do it alone. The stranger in town comes along, offering us an opportunity to let down our burdens and lighten our loads, but we refuse help. We see the weight of the world as "goods" that let the world know how strong we are, how useful we can be … just call us Ms. Independent and we wear that badge with a big chest full of pride. So, we walk onto crowded scenes stooped over and meeting the expectations of our comfort zones. So overburdened and distracted – trying to keep afloat so we don't tip over – that we've literally forgotten how to distinguish between which of the bundled packages are our original gifts, and which became baggage because others didn't want to carry their own weight and we've somehow managed to shoulder their share as proof of our womanhood. Others, in this sense, can be family and colleagues, but also in a larger context, can represent the society in which were socialized, and the cultural standards of our femininity within our own communities. If the cultural standard is to grin and bear it, it is not coincidental that great shame exists in not being able to do your part and live according to expectation of societal norms. There can even be a sense of embarrassment and even self-loathing to receive from the outside what you couldn't seem to achieve on your own.

SEEKING HELP.

We usually associate the word "stigma" with something negative. The *Oxford Dictionary*, which defines stigma as "A mark of disgrace associated with a particular circumstance, quality, or person,"[44] is not wrong in this association. Note the example sentence example: "The stigma of mental disorder." Well, that sure adds fire to the flames we're trying to extinguish!

As a strategically-thinking implementer, I've worked with a lot of women over the years who are visionary and full of heartwarming ideas. They enjoy sharing their knowledge, usually in a coaching or consulting capacity, or through informational products. Such individuals encourage women to become vulnerable and receptive to guidance for their journeys. But I noticed that, in time, many of these amazing professionals had been reluctant to do the same. Feeling a responsibility to be "the model," they could not be dealing with the same issues as the clients.

The most brilliant of the coaches were the ones who not only believed in the theories of their work, but also actively put those principles into practice – applying lessons learned to their own life circumstances regardless of whether or not they "made it" in their own professional journeys. Such consultants bled and cried, and shared that fact with their clients; rather than just speaking from a place of long experience, these professionals spoke from a place that said they were still learning and growing just like everyone else.

Here's the thing: when reaching certain levels of success, it's up to you to keep yourself in alignment with living and reevaluating your values, making adjustments, and forgiving yourself along the way. It's up to you to decide that no matter how you shaped everyone's opinion of yourself … you must give yourself permission to break the mold and *create who you need to be* for the next phase in your maturity, whatever that may be. While not glamourous, the process could very well entail starting over again upon realizing that the business you've built no longer fits in with the larger vision you now have … that, importantly, you didn't have before. It can even be a restart from something more basic (i.e. a medical crisis that changes your life and forever alters your business).

Despite the main culture, we become entrepreneurial in our opposition to the status quo, while yet still benefitting from the status quo of the culture in which we strive to create our movements.

To therefore balance the force of a movement toward shame and shame residue, to the best of our abilities we try to encourage people still suffering in silence to seek help, seek resources, seek support. The problem, however, when you're going through a depression – or when your anxious thoughts about impending doom weigh you down – is that sometimes, you're not really open to receiving aid of any kind.

CHAPTER 5

Suicide: That Final Destination Lingering in the Back of the Mind

Loneliness, all aloneness, trudging through
the desert, they call me a quiet storm.

Overwhelmed with paranoia, quicksand silencing
my screams of struggle, suffocation!

Not good enough, irrelevant, and worthless, it's like a deep dark
black hole, its gravitational pull sucking you into oblivion.

No one there, no one cares, and nothing really matters.

No! I'm relied on … but I'll let them down. No!
I'll fight for today … but I'm so tired.

So frustrated, can't do this anymore, fighting persistent
voices of "you're inadequate" … get out of my head!

Label me, teach me, grow me, use me, abuse me,
praise me, hate me, lift me, love me, leave me, don't

need me, please free me, I don't know me, but I'll
show me, just what it means to finally end me...
So much pain and what do I gain? Just another day?

— LYNETTE DAVIS, 2017 (A POEM EXPRESSING MY INTERPRETATION
OF THE MANY NARRATIVES ABOUT THE CRIPPLING EXPERIENCE
OF A DAILY STRUGGLE WITH MENTAL ILLNESS.)

DID YOU EVER JUST WAKE up one day and think: "Screw it all!" Maybe the night before you drank one too many glasses of wine to keep the negative thoughts away; perhaps you checked your emails upon that first upward extension of your eyelids, and knew it was a bad idea to open that one email that clearly looked like a verbal dissection. Maybe the whole darn month has just brought all fears about yourself to the surface: how you can't pay your bills; why you still have to eat ramen noodles and canned tuna every night for dinner; how you answer "Uh yeah, I'm in business for myself," when people ask if you work. And hoping they don't ask the real question, for which you have a big fat "no" response — which is, do you actually make money and a living from said business? Oh, and the scale is broken again because how the heck did you gain a pound from sleeping?!? Yup, "Screw it all!"

But still you roll out of bed, take a shower, grab the coffee, and wear the mask. Sometimes, though, you just can't do it anymore. One day becomes days, then weeks, then years, and before you realize it, you wake up and think: "I just can't go on like this anymore." "I just can't live with the nothing and no one I've become." For the entrepreneurially-minded person, that is the bat-signal to initiate change and innovate. But it's a different story for the person who is tired, and sick of being tired; for the person who tried and failed, and stopped believing the sweet words and promises of First World gurus;

or perhaps even for the person who actually did, by all society measures, succeed – but who just can't take the faking the funk anymore. For the people who just want the pain to stop … who in a wave of the white flag are ready to surrender after a long uphill battle that is the very hard work of living and loving and being free … for those who have had enough of never feeling enough, it's the final countdown. Death becomes a temptress promising the ultimate escape.

> *I have a very traumatic past. There's a history of abuse, parental suicide, and self-medication to cope with that abuse and family history. I've made several attempts over the years. It just felt like the only way out. With my last attempt, I felt responsible for all the people on my team and that I had failed them. I felt like I let everyone down, I had made all these promises and I thought "how dare I go back on my word." Everything about my life just felt like burden, I just…I just wanted everything to stop. – "Eleanor"*

There comes a time in every entrepreneur's journey for the question: "What am I really fighting for anymore?" It's totally possible to look up and around at what you've accomplished and the persona you've become in order to gain approval; recognition; a hefty paycheck; many options for a bed warmer; power and prestige – and think you've failed utterly and completely.

I can't capture the narratives of everyone who has ever contemplated suicide, and I most certainly cannot interview the dead and ask them, "So what was the final straw that broke the proverbial camel's back for you?" However, I can highlight the facts: according to the National Alliance on Mental Illness (NAMI), suicide is the tenth leading cause of death among adults in the U.S. and the second leading cause of death among people ages ten to twenty-four; furthermore, these rates are increasing.[45] I can also point out some typical warning signs, and direct you to people and advocacy groups who are actively working to decrease those statistics. Perhaps we can acknowledge and even back what's already working, and then (maybe somewhere down the line) humbly, yet vigilantly, allow the pre-drawn map of silent tears to guide our way to innovate in the arena of suicide prevention.

For now, let's get this important part out and in the open. You ready?

It is very rare that someone dies by suicide because of one cause. Thus, there are usually several causes, and not just one, for suicide.[46] — Kevin Caruso, Suicide.org

I agree and any Google search will tell you the same. There is no one major answer "why." We are complicated. With all our little idiosyncrasies, nothing about human existence has ever seemed so black and white. However, for the sake of having something to grasp: NAMI research has found that about 90 percent of individuals who die by suicide experience mental illness.[47] And according to World Health Organization (WHO), depression is a common mental disorder and one of the main causes of disability worldwide. Globally, an estimated three hundred million people are affected by depression; More women are affected than men.[48] The Anxiety and Depression Association of America states that nearly one-half of those diagnosed with depression are also diagnosed with an anxiety disorder.[49] Dr. Clack (referenced earlier) also reported, "…the majority of the people I see in my practice who have depression also have anxiety. I call them sister disorders."

Before I continue, I want to re-emphasize that there is no single cause for suicide. There are many factors that may put a person at risk for mental disorders, which are the most common conditions associated with suicide. But because this book explores entrepreneurship and people usually conduct businesses to make money, let's start there. Playing *Money* by Pink Floyd[50] may help set the mood for this section.

As mentioned in Chapter 1, the Money and Mental Health Policy Institute presented research that found if someone had a "major financial crisis" within the past six months, they are nearly eight times more likely to experience suicidal thoughts. Also, people with problem debt are twice as likely to develop major depression as those not in financial difficulty.[51] Now imagine always scrambling to make ends meet, pleading and begging to your higher power for a financial miracle so you can pay the mortgage or rent and not end up homeless. Or wondering how you're going to pay your vendors on time if your client decides to pay their invoice late, or worse, request a refund because you didn't deliver on the promises you never made her – but that she feels entitled to anyway. If you're thinking, "Well, if they're that bad with money then they don't need to be in business," let me remind you that businessmen who have filed bankruptcy have gone on to receive other chances to start other companies and even become leaders of countries. The point is, if every day feels like a mild or major "financial crisis" day because you "ain't got a pot to piss in" – how much do you think that affects one's esteem? How do you think such monetary uncertainty increases stress and anxiety levels on a daily basis?

I started my business on what they call a shoe string budget. Heck, I don't even think I had enough for a shoe string! Maybe "lint ball budget" is a better phrase? When I couldn't make ends meet after almost a year into the business, I began feeling dejected and inadequate in my business. It wasn't like I wasn't doing my best, because I was. Still I couldn't seem to catch a break. I just couldn't get the cash flow I desperately needed to make it work. I couldn't find a job either! With all the rejection, and debt piling up I felt so defeated. – "Tia"

Money of course isn't the be-all and end-all. Following are a few of the other factors that contribute to mental health conditions commonly shared by the women I interviewed.

MULTIPLE HEALTH CONDITIONS.

I've had several health issues come up that made it very painful for me to work for long periods of time in a day. I had to get on disability at one point, but that really isn't enough money to support myself. I'm educated, I'm a hard worker, so I know I can do more. I want to do more, but somedays it's really hard to even get out of bed. – "Jane"

TRAUMATIC EVENTS.

I was abused at a very young age, my mother had a disability and my father was an alcoholic and physically abusive. When my parents got divorced I was sexually molested by my stepfather. My first husband also abused me too. It became dangerous for me and my children to stay where we were. I eventually had the courage to leave my circumstance. I still carry that history with me. – "Eleanor"

FAMILY HISTORY.

Both of my parents struggled with depression; one of them decided to take their own life as a result. Because I had already been struggling with my own diagnosis, I felt like I already had a death sentence hanging over my head. – "Willow"

WORK-RELATED STRESS AND FEELING OVERWHELMED.

It's been really stressful. Witnessing people mock you, try to steal your creative ideas as if they were their own, always having to defend your place and position… Because of the type of business I have, I have to have a large presence on social media. If I'd say something that people don't agree with, if I posted the wrong thing they'd literally scream: "Go kill yourself!" – "Amaya"

THE AFTERMATH.

Even though death by suicide is probably not what one thinks about without certain factors coming into play, it happens. According to the research shared on the American Foundation for Suicide Prevention (AFSP) site, each year females attempt suicide three times more often than males; and every year 44,193 Americans die by suicide.[52]

Because of the stigma that still remains around mental illness and behavioral patterns that are designated as disorders (or in some instances, disorderly conduct), the notion of "taking one's own life" is often associated with attention-seeking, selfishness, and for those left behind in the aftermath … being unworthy of empathy and compassion.

Despite the negative association, suicide interestingly enough makes people wake up and pay attention – if even for a moment.

The intriguing aspect about the human experience is that regardless of which road we drive down, we each meet the same or surprisingly similar bumps. People living below the poverty line can experience traumatic symptoms like those of war veterans. Financially well-to-do people can have it all together until one of their children is suddenly in police custody due to an abrupt first-time episode of psychosis, later to be diagnosed with a schizoaffective disorder. Rich people can be broke(n) and poor people can lead rich lives through the wealth of happiness and joy beyond reason. The point is, mental health issues do not discriminate.

However, as Westerners we live in a society that judges which mental health issues are deserving of our consideration and which are issues of "those type of people." Because of this the reaction to death by suicide is either "what a shame, she was so talented and funny" or "I bet it was drugs, *those* people always…"

In business, we mourn the death of our fellow pioneers because entrepreneurs, even if hated, are often seen as people of potential (at least the ones with enough influence do). However, because of the potential of these "extraordinary ones," when such a peer dies "by their own hand" we also become overwhelmingly distraught. This hits very close to home for those who still struggle with managing their own mental health issues and fight earnestly to lead a fulfilling life.

Two close friends and colleagues of mine (in the tech startup scene) died by suicide … there were a lot of whispers about it for a while. Entrepreneurial people over here are under a lot of pressure. People focus on taking pills not so much mental health. My colleague was taking anti-depressants at the time he did it. That really had an effect on me because I already struggled with depression. I think those SSRI's can push people over the edge. There is a big problem with the healthcare industry in general, there just isn't enough education about alternative. But it doesn't help that people think I'm broken and need to be fixed. It's more like crisis intervention not health and healing…I think they felt really isolated like it wasn't OK for them to share how they feel. They didn't have people to let them know there are options and all of them are worth exploring. No matter how much success you have doesn't mean everything is wonderful inside. We need to talk about this so people are not alone. – M.A.

BUT WHAT IF I … YOU KNOW, JUST … NEVER EXISTED? The fact of the matter is suicide affects people in ways that are sometimes hard to convey. It is not surprising to see a cycle that goes something like this: we lose someone in our peripheral circle of connections; we then experience triggers; and we go through our own grieving process because death is real to us once again. Then we realize we've made it about ourselves; we feel guilty about it; we experience a loathing of sorts for making it about ourselves; then we jump back into action to distract our thought processes – which, by the way, is perfectly imperfectly human nature.

The very darkness that conquers one soul is the saving grace for another. Does this make one weaker than another? No, I don't believe so. As a matter of my strong personal opinion, it takes considerable strength to do that which is opposite of our supposed human predisposition, which is to survive. It also takes considerable strength to press on, to keep finding a reason to live – especially in the face of adversity. We all have different levels relative to the size of the crosses we can bear. We all are given different doors that lead us to different paths; some lead to life, some death, but most of the time there is a combination of both that represents the life, death, rebirth cycle that Pinkola Estés' *Women Who Run with the Wolves*[53] breaks down better than I could ever do it justice. And it is in that cycle of the pains of life, the unknowns of death, and renewal of rebirth that we are exposed to our own mirrors of truth.

Suicide became the truth for some while for others like myself, it became a warning bell, a reminder that if I did not implement a daily practice of consciously inviting spirit, purpose, and vision into my life I could easily yield to its seduction. During my own time in therapy, when I had a string of depressive episodes, my therapist asked me what kept me from wanting to take my own life. I answered that I was afraid of going to the Catholic school version of Hell. (Scary with a capital "S"!) I still questioned the existence of such a place, but because of my uncertainty, I didn't want to take a chance. (I had also been taught to believe that that's where I'd end up if I did indeed snuff out my own life.) Later I revealed that while I was too much of a wuss to die by suicide, I often wished I never existed. I wished God could make it so that I was never a manifestation of Divine imagination, that I would be erased from this mysterious Creator's memory and all the strings woven by lady fate. That way there would have never been a me to place on an Earth, Heaven, or Hell. When my therapist asked if I still felt that way, the me still in my twenties and going through a divorce answered honestly, "Yes."

I didn't know at the time that my thoughts were considered "passive suicidal ideation." Passive ideation can include scenarios like longing to die in your sleep, or hoping you'd get an "acceptable" disease like cancer and die "honorably" from that instead. Just because one doesn't intend suicide doesn't mean they won't set themselves up for active pursuit in the future. Many moons later and without a fear of Hell holding me back, the therapist asked again and I could finally answer (sarcastically, I admit): "Heck no, I'm soooo needed here." As

I write this today about ten years later (literally after having suffered all day from a severe acid reflux flare-up), I can honestly say I *want* to be here and that I am *purposed* to be here. The journey to get to this place of quiet contentment wasn't easy. It took plunging into the deep ocean that is my soul; becoming aware of the places that caused me so much fear; and having the courage to find the smallest, barely noticeable pathway to a warm ray of resolve that enabled me to swim through the muck and emerge on the other side.

COMING FACE TO FACE WITH THE SHADOW OF YOUR SOUL. I believe that there's a deep dark intensity behind the masks being worn, in order to keep people from seeing too much of what they don't want to see inside themselves.

I used to think that people were fake, with their plastered smiles, their limp handshakes, their dismissive glances, and their well-rehearsed elevator pitches. I think now those same people aren't even aware of what lurks in the shadows of their subconscious and because of that they are for all intents and purposes keeping it as real as their survival instincts allow. So real, that with each encounter they are truly a genuine and authentic expression of the self they've convinced themselves to be. If convincing themselves of a grandiosity as, and even better than, the next person at that particular encounter – that's the real self of that moment. We are tasked with seeing our own "shame triggers" so as not to be pulled in by someone living out their own.

Those of us with histories of mental and emotional health issues are probably just a bit more in touch with the shadows. On a "good" day it is our desire to work through them and find light at the end of the tunnel. Although – if we're really being honest – our first response to an exposure of shadow and darkness, which eventually manifests itself in some form of pain … is to cover the hurt and feel immediate relief.

But if we can somehow move through the tearing-down process which hinders the internal work required for our growth, and have a sort of renaissance within our psyche, we may find hidden meaning in our struggles. Meaning which gives us the strength to endure, the capacity to recover, and the drive to pursue ways to thrive and to expose pathways for others to do the same.

In the first lesson of *A Religion of One's Own*, Dr. Thomas Moore outlines one of his essential ingredients of home therapy, which I interpreted as self-help: go ahead, be courageous and tell your story. He goes on to write that "as you tell your stories, you may glimpse patterns you haven't noticed before. You may have small epiphanies and revelations. You may get insights into your situation."[54] I was very honored to be on the receiving end of those epiphanies and revelations. For as I conducted the research for this book through my interviews with women game changers, I could not believe just how amazing and beautiful these women were. How far they had come along, how brave it was of them to bare their souls to me, a complete stranger who just happened to have a fire in my belly for understanding the "why" behind the themes explored throughout this book. They shared, cried, and sighed, and they laughed a knowing laugh … the kind of laugh and sigh that only comes from a woman who has lived some and understood what Langston Hughes meant when he wrote *Not Without Laughter*[55] or what Maya Angelou meant in *I Know Why the Caged Bird Sings*.[56] And from their courage I found strength and resolve to write the truth as best I could, including my own, but not without a "shame resilience" plan in place.

CHAPTER 6

The Compelling Case for Compassion

*Compassion is not a relationship between the healer
and the wounded. It's a relationship between equals.
Only when we know our own darkness well can we be
present with the darkness of others. Compassion becomes
real when we recognize our shared humanity.*

*— PEMA CHÖDRÖN, THE PLACES THAT SCARE YOU:
A GUIDE TO FEARLESSNESS IN DIFFICULT TIMES, 2001*

THE ANTI-SUICIDE INITIATIVE KNOWN AS Project Semicolon came about as a way to say "my story isn't over yet." Many suicide attempt survivors wear a tattoo in solidarity to remember where they came from, perhaps where they don't want to go again, and as a beacon of hope to tell others that they too can live on and be the author of their story yet to be told. Sadly, the movement's founder, Amy Bluel, died by suicide; however, her legacy continues through the nonprofit she started and through the many pieces of wisdom she shared, including her personal narrative as a contribution to this book.

Perhaps by understanding the underlying messages in the narratives shared, we can identify the pieces that could have prevented tragedies such as Amy's death. Women have shared with me how out of control their emotions became; whether life seemed perfect or whether it was brewing a storm, they shared how they "contemplated suicide … but didn't go through with it."

THE WILL TO LIVE.

In the previous chapter I talked about the days where we want to give up. In this chapter, I want to look deeper into what makes us want to carry on.

Despite everything I've been through something in me didn't want to give up. I've had to reinvent myself several times throughout my life, and looking back, each experience has made me a stronger woman. Having people in my life that do care about me and do support me has helped pull me out of the black tar that kept trying to pull me under. — "Eleanor"

One day, I found myself lying on the floor sobbing with a lot of suicidal thoughts as usual. But for the first time I had people I was tied to and didn't want to leave them. I had two choices: put on my big girl panties or kill myself and be done with it. My newborn started crying and I got up to go comfort her. My choice was made, I had to stay with my baby. — "Jane"

After I tragically lost some family members I didn't think I could go on; the bottom fell out of the boat and I was drowning. However, after much urging and encouragement I went to therapy and was prescribed meds. Eventually I learned that a good psychiatrist will remove meds, release you from therapy and not string you along. I found a good psychiatrist who had the same end goal as me – healing. My whole experience led me to writing about my pain. Eventually, I wrote a book about my experiences which helped with the grieving process. There was wisdom to be gained and I wanted to help someone else who went through or is going through what I experienced. – "Tia"

A lot of women couldn't quite explain what particular factors kept them *wanting to live.* Some felt it was simply some ingrained characteristic, while others simply took things day by day ... and sometimes moment by moment. Because of that, I refer to organizations to help those of us who are advocates proactively put some puzzle pieces together. AFSP engages in five core strategies to prevent suicide, including: educational programs for professionals; promoting policies and legislation that impact suicide and prevention; and providing programs and resources for survivors of suicide loss and people at risk.[57]

One way to implement these strategies is to literally document each one and develop a list of ways to personally incorporate each strategy into your life and work ... the same way you would operate a business. After all, our health is our business. Likewise, it's important to note that preventing suicides depends not only on suicide prevention policies but also a healthy lifestyle, and an educated, supportive family and community.

While not every woman I interviewed had a documented suicide prevention kit, they all mentioned that the key to being able to get through the dark days was having a support system of some kind. Through listening to stories of women who presented themselves as very resilient by overcoming oppressive circumstances, I have also found that a strong support system was the common denominator. So, what makes for a strong support system? Well, for one, it requires connection.

THE IMPACT OF INTIMACY.

I knew I wasn't coping well with my mental health issues. I really isolated myself, but when I learned my daughter was struggling with depression too, I began checking on her. We now check in with each other. – "Eleanor"

The support person I had in my corner was also very business-oriented. She would tell me to "press through, it's gonna be alright"; [but] it felt like she didn't deal with her own issues and therefore couldn't identify with mine. I learned how unkind it is to tell someone to "get over it." Still, I didn't let that hinder me from reaching out. I learned you need different types of support for different areas in life. – "Tia"

I've always had some kind of support, which included my therapist, my 12-step recovery programs, etc. but the problem is when you are in depression, you're not open to receiving it. It's really a struggle, but it's really important to be vulnerable. You have to get on board with it and ask for support even as you question: "How can I be vulnerable without seeming weak?" I have colleagues who also run businesses while battling depression, we reach out to each other. – "Jane"

Support is necessary even if you're not experiencing depression. Ongoing support helps with awareness. Recognizing I'm fragile, recognizing it can be easy to go back into that downward spiral, recognizing triggers (like holidays, birthdays, etc.) is all a part of having the accountability of a support system. – "Amaya"

I had a great coach and mentor who worked with other clients who struggled with anxiety and depression. She helped me see that I expected too much of myself, that I was too critical of myself, and that I never felt accomplished. I learned to stop trying to be perfect, to breathe, to let things go. – "Willow"

Dr. Brené Brown's research found that women with high levels of shame resiliency reached out and shared their stories with people they trust.[58] I sensed in the women I interviewed that the intimate connection they felt with those whom they leaned on in time of emotional turbulence was of tremendous value to their well-being.

When I facilitate healing circles through the Love Yourself Love Your Business initiative – or as I like to call them, *"emotional liberation fellowships"* – I understand that the prerequisites for intimacy are trust, and a safe environment where women can be their most authentic selves. Intimacy in these fellowships takes courage, honesty with the self, and willingness to be in the moment to empathetically listen without comment (unless asked). However, intimacy can be a scary word for people. According to Hal Shorey, Ph.D., "Fearing intimacy and avoiding closeness in relationships is the norm for about 17 percent of adults in Western cultures.[59] "

Because of that, individuals need considerable courage to be intimate. It takes courage to be vulnerable enough to form healthy connections which require discernment and boundaries. Courageous women are the ones who reach out and share their experiences for the purposes of healing a culture of shame, one intimate conversation at a time. Our needing courage is something absolutely requiring awareness so that we can see the train of resistance coming and consequently get off the tracks. Otherwise we get hit with shame over and over again. Nelson Mandela once said that "courage was not the absence of fear, but the triumph over it."[60]And what I've learned from simply listening to stories is that courage is a habit to practice until it becomes your new normal.

When we are fueled by our courage to have something "real" with one another we create pathways to compassion. Dr. Brené Brown writes that "compassionate people are boundaried people" and that "the heart of compassion is really acceptance … if we really want to practice compassion, we have to start by setting boundaries and holding people accountable for their behavior."[61] It is a compassionate stance that helps us put an end to shaming others for their mental health conditions. Less shame equals greater chances of people seeking support. Compassion is important because not only does it foster a sense of inherit belonging, but also with that sense of self-worth it drives us to create a culture that holds people accountable as to how they treat their peers.

TO OPEN THE DOOR FOR MORE COMPASSION, START BY DEVELOPING EMPATHY.

I was talking with a mentor one day while writing this book and we exchanged stories about how we would team up and do a book tour together, talking about depression and entrepreneurship, each bringing our own unique perspective to the table. This mentor disclosed that she was indeed on medications for her own depression, and talked about how other people who also experienced depression but chose a non-pharmaceutical approach to their health and healing (or rather healing and ongoing upkeep of health) thought less of individuals using meds for the same ends.

Now, before proceeding I want to note that I am not anti-medication campaigner (though I personally chose not to take any meds for my own battle with depression). This is one major reason why I chose to interview as many women as possible, so that I could give you the truth as they saw it both individually and as a general consensus.

With that being said, I will state that I am an advocate for healing illness naturally. I have many friends who are tired of being sick all the time from medication side effects and no one backing them when they wish to see if they can be healthy without prescribed drugs. If someone wants to move beyond their meds, it makes sense to have the resources and systems in place to empower them to do so ... eventually and indefinitely if possible. However, as a part of that process I'd first require a thorough exploration of the root causes of the mental disorders. A second requirement would be a customized plan of action by medical professionals (such as holistic psychiatrists and practitioners of integrative and functional medicine, if you are in the position to work with them) who believe in a natural approach to healing, and are trained to make sure you're not stopping medications so prematurely that you end up relapsing right back into anxiety, depression or episodes of psychosis. *Third and most imperative is to have a strong support team in your corner,* and that that support team would include a psychotherapist.

I also believe you need to be your own best advocate; to be well-informed, start by tuning into virtual conferences like the Mental Wellness Summit (mentalwellnesssummit.com) or the Love Yourself Love Your Business Summit, (loveselflovebiz.com). I'm realistic enough to know everyone does not have access to the best healthcare coverage and has to work with what they got. I have many colleagues and friends who solely take medications so they can keep functioning and make it through their daily grind. According to investigators at Harvard Medical School, "Fewer than 20 percent of people on anti-depressants undergo psychotherapy, although it's often important in recovering from depression and avoiding recurrence."[62] With my own ego into play, I could not fathom why anyone wouldn't want to be optimally healthy – even if it requires more work than popping a pill. However, I can see why someone could not fathom digging up what triggered them into deep mental health conditions when a pill takes that type of pain away.

But back to the conversation with my mentor. Because I know that everyone has a different idea about what mental health recovery "should" look like, I had to pause when chatting with my mentor because I realized something very important ... we were all battling for mental health improvement but shooting each other down when we don't see things the same way. Mental health activists are in the forefront of opposing naysayers, fighting for mental illnesses to be taken as seriously as physical medical conditions. How can we unite to fight something so much larger than our differences of option? I decided that first we needed empathy.

Personally, I've had gut issues for quite a while. I finally did some research on what it could possibly be after a really painful attack that left me crying the night away, debating on going to the ER and deciding to clutch my poor tummy and try to sleep away the pain. My research led to information about conditions called GERD (gastroesophageal reflux disease) and gastritis. I didn't think I had either of those – and wouldn't know without seeing a doctor – but an educated guess led me to believe that whatever those people who *were* formally diagnosed were eating to get better would probably do me justice ... even if I didn't actually have the two medical conditions. I had been taking NSAIDs for far too long for the killer cramps I struggled with years before, and there was a great chance my stomach lining was jacked up because of it. So, I went gluten-free, dairy-free, caffeine-free, and basically flavor-free. A frustration-fueled diet because I had to say goodbye to the garlic, tomatoes, and cayenne pepper I so loved. I went from eating yummy exotic dishes and at least one sweet tea a day to "meh."

However, after about two weeks on the new diet I felt tremendously better both physically and emotionally; I even lost some weight. But when week four of my menstrual cycle came around I struggled … a lot. Even though I was given a suggestion for alternative meds to avoid the offending NSAID pills I had been on since age thirteen, the poor replacement pills wore off after a mere two hours and I was in horrible pain. Frankly, I didn't give a flying dragon about how the pills were only treating the symptoms, how they were making me sick and probably killing me slowly, how the pharmaceutical companies were the "man" and holding me down. I only wanted the pain to go away, far, far away so I could go about with my day to day existence right then and there.

Talking to my previous mentor reminded me of my own personal battles with handling a medical condition. Even though it's not the same experience I understood the very urgent need to just get through the day, to just make it to the next moment. I also knew from experience that despite medical confirmation, some would even argue that PMS and cramps are a figment of my imagination – but despite what anyone thought or what any doctor concluded my pain was very real to me.

If I was going to talk about a need for empathy and compassion, I wanted an understanding that everyone is entitled to choose a path of healing that may not be in alignment with what we individually believe to be the "right" method. We don't need to put one another down to further prove that our choice is the better or best way. Again, even though I've never taken antidepressants I completely understood where my mentor was coming from. I purposely and intentionally looked for ways in which I could relate, while not sacrificing my belief system that we could one day find hope and healing beyond our prescriptions. While I look forward to the day when my natural and holistic means of treatment will be considered mainstream rather than alternative, I understand the urgency one feels to get rid of pain as quickly as possible.

TIME TO KICK OLD HABITS TO THE CURB.
However, empathy isn't an easy feat. Someone says the right thing to push the right buttons and we get irritable, or defensive, or maybe even aggressive. The point is when we become triggered, we react. We say things we don't mean, we have conversations when we are hurt and angry. With so much going on in our lives, we don't think to take action unless it hits close to home. Does that make us heartless? Does that make us selfish? I don't believe so. I think it makes us human. We have so much stimuli at our disposal, that we prioritize life as needs rise to the surface and can no longer be ignored. But what if we were more aware of our habits and instinctual reactions?

You don't know what you don't know … and that's scary for some of us. Why? Because it brings us closer to the realization that we as humans are flawed and fallible. Flawed and fallible means that we will indeed make mistakes; mistakes translate into failures and distorted thinking says that a failure means you're a failure. See what's wrong here? If we aren't understanding and forgiving of ourselves, what kind of expectations are we placing on others? What I've learned in my interviews with business owners who reported being successful despite their history with conditions such as depression and anxiety is that where most people are trying to avoid feeling the pain of failure, they embrace it as a natural part of their life cycle. I'd even go as far to say they anticipate that at any moment in their current cycle of loving their life and business, the tides could turn and no longer be in their favor. And because they are aware of that possibility, they move forward along their journey despite fear and in as much awareness of the present moment as possible. It is because of their persistent awareness of their human nature that they are less stressed about what was and less anxious about what could be. As a result, they are also more apt to have healthy boundaries and realistic expectations of others.

Compassion then becomes an intentional reactive stance. I'd like to believe that we have all to some extent experienced compassion enough to have a grasp of what it means. What if instead of only reacting to mental health issues due to being able to relate personally or attributing those concerns to someone who means something to you, we react with compassion simply because we know that no one wants to be labeled as "other"?

How much less anxious can we be if we already expect that mistakes do and will occur? No doubt about it, someone is going to have a meltdown, someone is not going to have their head 100 percent in the game, your right-hand assistant, COO, or vice president of "everything" isn't always going to execute your vision perfectly. And you know what? You as a leader are going to have days when you're feeling off-kilter too. Because of these realities, we take a step back and breathe. We remember that people want to be seen as human and not as a commodity for production. You remember that you want to be seen as a human and not solely that founder or president, or CEO who did this or made that. We then develop ways of operating that instill the importance that everyone under our leadership, stewarding, guidance, or direction are just as worthy of being as we are. Why? Because people who feel worthy of being will fight for their lives. Let me phrase this in a more clinically correct way: Promoting the emotional and social well-being of others leads to increased lifespan.

A COMMITMENT TO CONNECTEDNESS AND COMPASSION BUILDS RESILIENCE.

I think entrepreneurship affords us a very unique view of life. We take risks in life just like entrepreneurship, and from a healthy and worthy stance we accept failure, we cope, we dust ourselves off, and keep on moving. None of this is easy, and all of this is work for anyone. Because we struggle with perception, those of us with mental health disorders tend to need some extra help in the form of treatment and ongoing recovery strategies so that we too can live fulfilling, resilient lives. Resiliency has been defined by the American Psychological Association as:

> ...the process of adapting well in the face of adversity, trauma, tragedy, threats, or significant sources of stress – such as family and relationship problems, serious health problems, or workplace and financial stressors. It means "bouncing back" from difficult experiences. Research has shown that resilience is ordinary, not extraordinary. People commonly demonstrate resilience. Being resilient does not mean that a person doesn't experience difficulty or distress. Emotional pain and sadness are common in people who have suffered major adversity or trauma in their lives. In fact, the road to resilience is likely to involve considerable emotional distress. Resilience is not a trait that people either have or do not have. It involves behaviors, thoughts and actions that can be learned and developed in anyone.[63]

To me, resiliency is the ability to rise again like the sun after a long journey, grappling to find your way through the dark cold nights. The mythical phoenix rebirth "out of the ashes" story symbolizes the essence of resiliency, for in order to be reborn there is a burn. I also find the butterfly to be resilient as well: to first crawl around on its belly, having the belief of being so much more when it has never known itself to be anything but; to then to do the work of building a cocoon (a dark place of rest and confinement); going through an all-consuming transformation while in that dark place; then having to fight some more to get out of that cocoon; and finally flying into the sky in a new form, with new vision.

So how do businesswomen build up entrepreneurial roller coaster resilience?

For anxiety, repeating [the] mantra "I am at peace" and getting centered with that thought means getting present [in the] moment. You are then empowered to think and choose differently so that fear doesn't take over. If you are saying that mantra, you are using the phrase "I am" – you are connecting to the divine in you. You are connecting to your intuition. And peace means you aren't going back to the past where you're letting some experience haunt you or the future where you're worried about how something is going to turn out. In the present, you cannot let the past become you. Being centered and in the present moment you're empowered to create or direct your future more. Being centered means being aware, not blindly ignoring the negative, or not being upset. It's about being aware enough to choose thoughts that support you. "So okay, this is negative ... what does this mean?" Because being positive while shoving the negative in a closet isn't centered. – E.V.

I've been in mental health recovery and have many years of sobriety. After everything I've been through, I know that I have to take care of myself. I need to maintain balance because I know I can be thrown off easily. So, I pace myself by meditating. Through this practice it's easier for me to notice when things aren't quite right. It helps me to "be in the now" rather than focus on my failures. – M.M.

I've learned that it's my job to say "no." I'm not ever going to be interested in carrying a platter. I want a salad plate and I have to know just how much I can put on that plate. There's a fine balance between perfectly busy and too busy. We overwhelm ourselves as entrepreneurs, if we can just take a step back and breathe knowing that none of us escape having a "mental health" moment we learn to build in safe guards even at an executive level. I literally block times on my calendar. So if I see I don't have time for me, something isn't right. – J.T.

I practice self-care. I reach out and ask for support when I need it. I develop friendships with people who respect my boundaries. I take time for myself, and eat well. I make it my business to know what I need to stay healthy. – D.D.

Why is resilience so important to business? Leadership coach Andréa Ranae of AndreaRanae.com shares that we can look at resilience "as the capacity of the community around a person to be able to support them. In this way, a resilient person asks for support. They are able to move forward through difficult situations or obstacles, but they don't expect themselves to do it alone. They see conflict as an opportunity for growth and relationship building. They're willing to be uncomfortable especially if it moves them toward growth." The movement towards growth typically requires change. In case you didn't know, the climate for business is almost always changing.

FOUNDATIONS FOR CHANGE.

Resiliency essentially is about adapting to change. Change, without a doubt, starts within. It is work for which we have to be up to task. Sometimes, we don't realize *how* up to task we are until we are forced into circumstances that challenge our way of thinking and seeing the world. In addition, we as humans are groomed to be social beings, connected in ways that can enhance our growth and prepare us for the work we have to do for character and circumstantial metamorphosis.

> *I was always surrounded by strong women who fought really hard to get what they felt was worth it and for what they believed in. When obstacles came their way, they took them on head-on. They may have wanted to run away, but they were raised to believe nothing in life came free and so they had very little expectations of simply being handed privileges. Did I willingly embrace obstacles? Absolutely not! But I realized that years and years of watching these fighters and survivors made me more prepared to be fighter and survivor too. – "Tia"*

If nothing else, I've learned this from interviewing women entrepreneurs: those who are able to stay afloat in life and business despite their history with mental illness – and actually thrive – had support systems in place that they felt comfortable enough to be vulnerable with. Furthermore, they also had some kind of self-love practice in place (whether they understood it as such or not).

In alignment with the most popular and sound research, exercise – which would fall under self-care in the self-love paradigm – would without a doubt be a priority. However, people keep talking about the importance of exercise because it is one of the toughest daily practices to get individual affected by mental illness to do. So, I looked for a pattern of habits that most interviewees felt was easily accessible and feasible; the self-love practice that was most present was the simplest, but probably the most important – and certainly in my opinion the first step to recovery and healing … namely, self-awareness. Almost all of my interviewees had mechanisms to alert when they were a "yellow light zone" four to six on a scale of one to nine, nine being the healthiest, most loving versions of themselves.

The starting place for change is first and foremost understanding ourselves enough to know when we are feeling off-center and out of balance.

To "know thyself" is a huge undertaking. However, it is our responsibility to master ourselves; to have an intimate relationship with who we are at our core. By doing so we are better able to recognize when that core is shaken. I don't write that to make anyone feel ashamed, but as a way to acknowledge that far too many people (including people who lead others) hand that responsibility off to someone else, something else. Furthermore, beyond simply knowing, we have to make a choice to want to heal. Yes, mental illness can debilitate, but we have to believe that we can heal, and then follow that up with a commitment to action that aids in our recovery process. These are important steps to take if we are going to partake in this lifetime journey to maintain our well-being. It is through this commitment to action that we become acquainted with resistance, yet by overcoming resistance we grow, and in our growth we are strengthened, enabling us to build foundations for transformation.

Transformed lives collectively and when unified create change in culture. In her eye-opening TEDx talk about gender roles in society, author Chimamanda Ngozi Adichie says, "Culture does not make people. People make culture."[64] If the workplace is based on a culture of health and well-being, which then produces a healthy and well workforce that happens to be essential for prosperity, how much better off would the world be? How much more in our business prowess could we achieve if our mission was truly changing the world (hopefully in the direction of peace, equity, and all that positive psychology jazz)? How powerful a statement it is to say as a leader, "This is the type culture I will drive because the status quo of shame and stigma does not make me or my company, or determine how we deliver our services and/or products"? Why not have a conscious business with an evolving culture, one that doesn't subscribe to old ways of doing things because "that's how business was always done"? But before I go full-blown into grandiose dreams of a seemingly impossible feat, let me back up for a bit and talk about the pulse of transformed lives and businesses.

CHAPTER 7

The Transformative Power of Love in Business (and the Importance of Creating a Culture that Fosters Workplace Wellness)

*A woman is the full circle. Within her is the
power to create, nurture and transform.*

*– Diane Mariechild, Mother Wit:
A Feminist Guide to Psychic Development, 1981*

HERE'S THE THING ABOUT SIMPLE concepts and ideologies: they're too basic! They are so basic in conclusion, that they piss us and our complicatedness off. People who are really into spirituality are too much heart and not enough brain. And science "that is illogical" people are too much in their heads and out of touch with their emotions. Then there's business people … who are trying to make the world go around to the beat of their own drum. When any side presents a simple way to view the other's world it's unbearable. It strips the other of their self-righteousness and, well, we just can't have that. Therefore, I am not surprised that when anyone presents classic guidelines and principles interpreted for a mindset contrived in westernized society, people go "well duh, that's a given" or "that's to be already understood." My take is, if one is stating the obvious why are we still stuck crying, bemoaning, and groaning about the same stuff generation after generation? It seems that we are all still babes in this thing … this awakening to the truths of our human nature and the function or dysfunction of our brains. If the drivers of commercialism are allowed to study what makes us tick and what gives us pause, what makes us inspired to act out of self-preservation in the struggle for survival – and then at every opportunity throw it in our face so they can keep getting our dollars as we engage in (always temporary) subconscious attempts to fix ourselves. Well, why not then constantly talk about the things that do in fact work as a way to resist that which means us more harm than good? You've officially been given a fair heads-up of my approach within this chapter!

Grammy Award-winning singer Patti LaBelle crooned over the car stereo about her sweet love[65] long before a guy on YouTube bragged about her sweet potato pie baking skills.[66] The song was one of many "romantic love" songs on the *Waiting to Exhale* movie soundtrack. I chose to reference this because I feel that most us of women are holding in so much angst, trying "to do" while waiting to exhale so we can simply experience the breath of life and "just be". In this sense, "being" isn't about stagnation, or passivity, it's about recognizing the "awe" factor in ourselves and in the world around us. The simple things. By doing so, we can move away from our frenzied, anxious and unrealistic expectations about how we should show up in the world and to whatever audience we've convinced ourselves require ongoing standing ovation performances – day in and day out, night after "one glass of wine" night. Essentially, just being is a simple awareness, a conscious awareness … but it is not easy because you know we "get in our feelings," lost in our restless inner chatter, and we're "busy and stuff." Hence ancient wisdom lends us "the way out" of our complexities to the simple art of being. From monotheist and new age spiritual teachers to atheist and agnostic philosophers, all saying "just love." That's what they offer us …love. Of course, we either turn away from or run with love, since the emotion keeps coming up anyway. However, when we run with love we make it complex and confusing and profitable, and finally ungraspable to the point that we convince ourselves how unattainable and unrealistic and even foolish it is to even reference love in anything we want taken seriously.

Okay, so let's talk about what can be taken seriously, the influence of the arts and media on people. Don't believe me? Go look up "most visited grave sites" on a search engine. You will find a lot of creative types in the results. In this day and age, musical pop stars get paid hefty sums just to appear on an ad for a beverage, because that's how influential they are to mainstream audiences. When England's Prince William specifically called American pop star Lady Gaga to talk about and collaborate on a mental health initiative, people tuned in.[67] Great … but we're not pop stars and some of us don't have the likes of Lady Gaga as a Facetime contact. No worries! That's not why I mentioned this. The point is the type of messages they share knowing they have a platform, and that they're on to something. With seeming effortlessness, creative types compose outward expressions of what's going on inside our heads – even if a bit misconstrued at times.

Consider that The Beatles sang "All You Need Is Love," [68] and then years later fellow British musician and composer Elton John wrote a book about combating the stigma of HIV/AIDS entitled *Love Is the Cure*.[69] People pay attention. And pop stars aren't the only ones having these types of conversations. Want to know what floats around on social media besides cat memes? Personal narratives about love lives or the lack thereof! If people have someone to listen, whether it be a Twitter following, or YouTube subscribers, they are speaking, ranting, sharing their experiences about their concept of love. We are given the impression that if there is love, we cannot go wrong. If there is love, everything will be well within ourselves and inevitably the world. It sounds so simple that in fact it's pretty much glossed over, or met with a roll of the eyes by anyone who knows what the phrase "woo-woo" means. However, when hearing certain phrases repeated I sometimes get curious enough to look deeper into them. Why would we say such a thing? What does it really mean? Who does it truly benefit in a society if we pass this type of information around? Is it helping or harming those who receive such messages? I suppose it depends on the intention of the one telling the story, and what they're motivated by when spreading their ideas.

The intent to cure.

> *Love is the cure,*
> *for your pain will keep giving birth to more pain*
> *until your eyes constantly exhale love*
> *as effortlessly as your body yields its scent.*[70] *— Rumi*

One of the many motivating factors to continue on with this book – when I seriously wanted to call it quits – was to say with confidence to whomever is reading: that you are not broken; that your colleague is not broken; that your employee or contractor is not broken; that your family member, friend, and fellow entrepreneur is not broken. I couldn't wait to write with all of my heart that "I see you." To reassure you that you are not alone. Born with or socialized into your mental health condition(s) does not earn you an automatic nomination for the "fix me" awards. Living with illness or living without illness boils down to the same raw element ... living. If we can, living long and prospering. And by "live" I mean live with the knowledge of what it really means to be "cured." Since that's what we're seeking, right? A cure to the everyday problems associated with living.

What would a "cure" look like for mood disorders or other issues associated with behavioral health? Is this cure in and of itself a subjective solution when it comes to state of mind, emotions, and behaviors? Let's say that someone decided that their version of "cured" is that they're "happy all the time," and so with the intention to stave off their own fears of not having enough joy to fit in somewhere and be accepted, someone else creates a simple sapphire-hued pill that will put one person in an endless happy state. Then perhaps another person will make a different pill of azure tone that accelerates the maximum capacity of the brain, and with it comes money and security, all of this to satisfy another person's version of "cured." So, we take our pills to manipulate our brain functioning into constantly believing that everything is awesome, enabling us to see nothing but utopian standards of living no matter what's going on in the "real world." Is being in a state of elevated mood and ecstasy our true aspiration as human beings? Since there have been numerous "say no to drugs" campaigns over the years, I'm going to guess not. Being the huge sci-fi fan that I am, between movies like *The Matrix*[71] and *Serenity*,[72] it also seems that even if these sapphire and azure pills weren't recreational and the U.S. Food and Drug Administration approved, there is always one human (or many) who is not too keen on being a puppet and would feel that any brain manipulation is doing just that. So, if not on a magical land inside our minds where we dwell in eternal happiness, and we simply do what we do, whether pill-induced or not ... in order to have the capacity to perhaps be "normal" are we then cured? If so, what then is normal human conduct and who gets to define it – and what is their aim?

This is why social behavior was always so fascinating to me. With or without pills to treat us, people scour the web, try out different religions, look to leaders, shuffle into clinician offices looking to be cured of whatever ails them in life. Perhaps we'd like to be rid of our horrific flaws, our brutal personalities, our endless tears, our sleepless nights, our constant worries of abandonment, our persistent thoughts of leaving supposedly menial existences. Or maybe we're tired of looking out onto the horizon and seeing an endless sea of societal problems, and not being clever or rich or powerful enough make any changes. Essentially, some of us are looking to be normal (usually in order to blend in and/or be accepted for survival purposes), some of us are looking to be pretty close to perfect, and for many, a pain-free life sounds very appealing. But before I go down an endless rabbit hole, let's take a quick look at the linguistics of the word "cure."

"Cure" as we have come to know it from the Original Middle English (as a noun) derives from the Old French *curer* (verb), *cure* (noun), and both originate from the Latin *curare*, "take care of," or *cura* "care." As the original noun's meanings included **"care, concern, responsibility,"**[73] how interesting it is that when we talk about "cure" the concept is presented as if it's a onetime deal. "She's found the cure! We're all saved!"

Let's break this down further, shall we? *Care* (verb) means to "look after" and provide for the needs of.[74] *Concern* means to "be about"[75] and *responsibility* speaks about "having a duty to deal with something."[76] When I read those definitions, I understand that there is some kind of action or occurrence taking place in the context of those meanings. If I've learned only this about life, it's that life is a series of actions and occurrences. If that is the case, then the recipe for living a "cured" human existence is about the ongoing care, concern, and responsibility for our well-being. And if we're going to really take a deep look at the intent of the cure, the aim is the well-being of our spiritual nature – the essence of consciousness. Simply put, we are caring for the "I" in order to move from saying things like "I am tired of myself" to "I love myself."

Curing ourselves presents us with a unique opportunity to be intentional and, dare I say, disciplined in the art and subsequent ongoing practice of living and working from a place of health, healing, and wholeness. Dr. Clack states that "Healed means you got healing for a particular part of your life, you don't stop doing what got you there. You upgrade your level of choices to continue healing because healing is a lifelong process. There is ALWAYS going to be something to come up in life." This ongoing care, concern, and responsibility – which is how we cultivate wholeness – is where love, and authentic expressions of love, come into play.

LOVE THE CONCEPT, LOVE THE ACTION.

I wanted to drop the stylistic approach employed up to this point, make this last chapter about something else, and conclude with concepts that are more businesslike (if there is such a thing). I wanted to present the kind closure that offered upwardly mobile "steps to success" with a simple formula, but … love called and I chose to answer while fully awake and aware of how it might be received. As someone who uses methodical thinking skills honed when obtaining my social science degree, to study love from a psychosociological perspective, I understand that even if I conclude that love is not only the cure, but possibly the ultimate reality – we need to agree about how love works in deeply meaningful, yet practical ways. Also, it would be a disservice to you if I did not present some concrete examples on the role of love in suicide prevention and as a contributor to ongoing healing for individuals who have platforms and are positioned to influence.

Abstract concepts about some sunshine and rainbows bursting out of your purse simply won't work. Basically, what I'm saying is that a theory of love needs to be fused with something we can wrap our minds around in order for us to "get it" or, rather, for us to see how love touches our lives right here and now and/or affects our bottom-line. Since we like to do and get matters done to move forward (and not feel useless in society), let's start with the concept of "love is as love does."[77]

I've heard some variation of this concept throughout my life. The most popular being "love is a verb." But I read about this particular phrase (i.e. "love is as love does") in the book *The Road Less Traveled* by Dr. M. Scott Peck. The concept is exactly as it sounds: about exertion, both intention and action; about a conscious choice. When it comes to business, this passage resonated the most "Love is not simply giving; it is judicious giving and judicious withholding as well… It is leadership." He goes on to write that "love is a form of work or a form of courage."[78] I'd go further and say that love is the courageous work it takes to maintain the health of a business.

In *All About Love: New Visions*, author bell hooks reiterates the work of Dr. M. Scott Peck and adds that with love, "work could have a different meaning and focus." She understood that cashflow and making a profit was important (especially if you want to remain in business) but that they don't "take precedence over valuing and nurturing human life and well-being."[79] However, in order to choose love we'll have to have the courage to confront and move through our fears. Sociologist and Life In Focus Coaching founder Kesha Moore, Ph.D. wrote, "All human behavior and thoughts are propelled by one of two motivations: love or fear. These motivations are mutually exclusive, meaning that both cannot occupy the same space (thought/behavior) at the same time." Why is this so important? Dr. Moore writes that "…to the extent that a behavior is motivated by love, it will produce life, growth (prosperity), and well-being (health and harmony). Yet, if that same behavior or thought is motivated by fear, it will produce sickness, stress and disease."[80] So how do we use the motivation of love rather than fear to make well-being a priority in the workplace?

HEALTH AND WELLNESS IN THE WORKPLACE, WHETHER A SOLOPRENEUR OR CEO AT A LARGE CORPORATION.

"And the beauty of wholeness which is the root meaning of the word health, healthy, healing, and holy is this sense that we may already be integrated, we may already be whole."[81] – Jon Kabat-Zinn

This is where the "something we can wrap our minds around" part of the equation comes in. Gallup reports that only 13 percent of employees worldwide are fully engaged at work and only 29 percent in America.[82] At the time of the writing, "workplace wellness" was finally becoming a *thing* for corporations. Current research suggests that workplace culture can influence health outcomes. According to the people over at The Center for Association Leadership, "Healthier employees make for a stronger association. If you're looking to build a workplace with more staff camaraderie, greater productivity, and less absenteeism, an organization-wide wellness initiative can help you get there."[83] Well, wouldn't it make sense that leaders of companies and their managerial teams also need to be healthy for the sake of business growth and success factors?

Wellness programs were always around on some level, but once the phrase became more recognizable companies began seeking out consultants to help them incorporate it into their place of business. So, I too sought out a consultant to help me paint a picture with words on how wellness programs can work in business.

Colleen Brigid Fitzpatrick, LCSW and founder of Instrumental Change, LLC says that "Workplace wellness (organizational psychology) is the integration of physical and emotional health programs in work. The approach is usually to be preventative and proactive rather than reactive. Some more traditional examples of such programs are: Weight Watchers™ (at work), and the employee assistance program (EAP). The goal of a workplace wellness program is changing [the health of the] workforce [for the better]. For issues like mental health a program may look to address reasons for absenteeism and loss of productivity." Programs can also incorporate thinking outside-the-box about how we view traits we find undesirable. A workplace wellness consultant can work companies to reduce turnover by "looking at negative traits and seeing them as perfect for specific jobs. Sometimes that means movement to departments that fit [a particular individual] better. For example, Microsoft launched a job placement program to specifically hire people living with autism." Fitzpatrick believes the success of wellness programs "starts with looking from the top down (leaders have to believe [in] it first). We're talking about team building: managers monitor[ing] people [to identify] leaders [who] inspire them; then look[ing] at employee interest[s] (flex time, work from home one day a week, health screenings, mindfulness meditation, etc.) … actions have to match what you say as a leader."

Below are a few different perspectives of how workplace wellness programs can work, and realistic obstacles faced revealed by the narratives shared.

VIEWPOINT OF AN EXECUTIVE LEADER:
"I have had both successes and failures with implementing wellness programs.

"My philosophy with any environment I go into is that we work hard and play just as hard. So, I encourage staff to be playful and supportive of one another. Cattiness and backbiting are not tolerated as these behaviors have a highly negative impact on the organizational culture and its mental/environmental health."

Successes:

- "At least once per quarter we had stressless afternoon. That meant that staff spent the afternoon playing. The activities could be a fun silly board game, movie and popcorn, etc. I did not participate in these since my presence tended to change the dynamic and staff did not feel as free to 'let loose.' The events took place in the conference room and I could hear them laughing all the way upstairs in my office."
- "Every year we did an outing at the park. We had an independent contractor who worked with us who was also a [physical education] teacher, so she was in charge of getting us all moving with fun activities and competition."
- "Once a year we also did a 'fundraiser' for the agency. The activity was to bring stuff from home you didn't use or want – we would then auction the items off. We often raised [over eight hundred dollars]. One year, we auctioned my baking. I baked a cake or two per month – any cake anyone wanted. These activities build team [morale], relaxed all, and also promoted staff to be more invested in the organization."
- "Servant leadership is an important aspect of any wellness program – my staff knows that what they need comes before anything I need to do AND that I will not ask them to do anything I am not willing to do myself.

* "Fitness – I am now in the process of developing a fitness type program for one of the agencies I work with. Fitness is not defined as simply physical, but all types of fitness. We are looking at emotional/mental health, financial, physical, nutrition, etc. The intent is to support staff who feel under stress in an organization that has been in crisis or transition for more than a year."

Challenges:

* "The biggest challenge in my mind is motivating staff who are not willing or interested or trusting enough to be motivated. All the best programs in the world will not succeed if the participants are disengaged and apathetic. I had this experience in one environment where no matter what I tried, staff were simply too disengaged or, in retrospect, scared."
* "Leadership team– if the leadership team does not buy into the concept of wellness they themselves will sabotage the process and, conceivably, make things worse."

– P.A.

VIEWPOINTS OF SEVERAL STARTUP FOUNDERS:

We hired a personal trainer who comes to the office twice a week for anyone who wants to participate in a group workout. It's so much fun. – A.K.

We created a company that helps other startup founders find a yoga teacher to teach at their offices for 1 hour during lunch or after work. We had great feedback and believe that it can really boost productivity levels and employee satisfaction. – M.B.

I try to stay ahead of the stressors, accept situations, and the fact that I can't control [everything]. – R.S.

VIEWPOINTS OF FREELANCERS, SMALL BUSINESS OWNERS, AND MICRO ENTERPRISE OWNERS:

Talk therapy sessions and daily journaling are my go-tos. – V.F.

I find it's important to do something different and cultivate your identity outside your work activities. – E.C.

There are five things I want to cover in my world: health, wealth, space, spirit, and mind. So, I try to do something every day that fits into those 5 areas. – B.M.

I started doing Zentagles after I learned it helps people with emotional issues such as depression. It is even good for vets! – M.M.

I volunteer at an animal shelter once a week. It's very therapeutic for me. –T.A.

I personally have a document of business standards that make health and wellness a priority. My operational standards include self-love breaks every business day. My theory is if people can take fifteen minutes for a cigarette break at their corporate gig, then I can take fifteen minutes to dance, walk around the block, meditate, write affirmations, or read a spiritual text.

EMBEDDING THE WORK OF LOVE INTO YOUR BUSINESS. So now that's we've glimpsed some examples of how we can implement wellness initiatives into our company cultures, you may be asking, "What does love have to do with transforming business and how does this all related to workplace wellness"? In the last chapter, I briefly touched on resilience, mentioning how good coping skills and support systems was important for adapting to the climate of change we cannot escape in business. Now, I want to touch on a really practical concept about resilience in the workplace. According to author and Conner Partners founder Daryl R. Conner: "…we can also think of resilience as a property of organizational systems. The overall leadership of the organizations (its vision, mission, and strategy, and its culture), can both reflect the elements of resilience and support them."[84] I want to apply what he says about resilience in a business context by approaching it with a disposition for and commitment to love. We can think of love as the core of all organizational systems. This includes the mini-systems we develop for business operations. And within each system, love in action is the primacy of the functioning that drives the interconnected parts. So, whatever workflow methodology we choose to leverage for optimal business growth, love is the foundation that ties everything together. Whatever workplace wellness program we incorporate into our culture, love is the glue that helps strategy, productivity, and profitability stick. In "Our Highest Calling: Love Suffused Work," Jo-Ann Triner, an adviser to the Institute for Research on Unlimited Love, purports that:

> …love for our fellow man generates a self-sustaining energy that no management team can artificially create. It draws energy from our center that is the very wellspring of vitality, passion and purpose. Such world-class work requires no prompting, no cajoling and no incentives. It operates from a

place so sacred that even the most menial work is transformed with meaning, subtlety and nuance.[85]

Therefore, while we incorporate wellness initiatives into our operations in order to have less absenteeism (mentally and physically), and greater productivity, we also incorporate it because a culture "of oneness rather than sameness,"[86] as Eric Fromm says, is a way to foster authentic connectivity with each other. We have the courage to take the path not too often traveled. We set out to develop a workplace culture where we see each other as whole; separate as unique individuals, yet interconnected. We do that by incorporating practices that cultivate compassion such as mindfulness. We set standards to be respectful of one another, understanding and forgiving due to differences, while looking for ways to value those differences because we realize what each difference brings to the table. In this instance, love then manifests as creativity. Creativity breeds innovation. In this sense, it's about changing behaviors. Just like love, innovation is an active process that works if we work at it while challenging ourselves to think differently. The practice challenges us to look at old ways of being and doing, and to create something new.

Let me give you a small example of how love can work in a workplace setting. In my own effort to embed love into every facet of my human existence, I persistently maintain my own mental health through deliberate spiritual practices alongside traditional recovery work like seeing therapists or participating in support groups. Many times, I don't want to take concerted actions involved with maintaining my recovery, but I cannot expect to feel connected to anyone else if I feel disconnected within myself. Do I execute perfectly with each attempt? Of course not! But as long as I have breath in my body, I will keep on with the keeping on.

And guess what? I'm fully aware that it's easier said than done. But because of my awareness, I am better prepared to handle the obstacles I encounter along my wholehearted journey. While writing this book both a close friend and relative were hospitalized. One for treatment of cancer, and the other for treatment of a couple of mental illnesses. I of course had to continue working while trying to offer support to my family (and I considered all parties and their families my family because of our shared history, blood relation or not). I'd like to say I wasn't affected by the events taking place, because I felt either numb or indifferent, but I realized those reactions were a part of my own defense mechanisms to hide away the hurt and sense of loss I was feeling. I was already in a grieving process – just not really understanding what was happening. I was eventually able to recognize my feelings because I practice cultivating a state of quietude, to eventually contemplate how I'm seeing myself and the world around me through nature walks, hatha yoga, and journaling. However, colleagues and clients are not mind readers and do not know that I am grieving. It is my choice on whether or not to share my personal life with them, as ours is a professional relationship. It is also up to me to put resources in place to keep myself from taking my hurt and pain out on my contractors, and allowing that to hurt my work performance. This is why with the aid of my business coach, I built and documented standards as foundational cornerstones of my practice, and I work on my self-worth to honor them because emergencies do happen whether we invite them into the atmosphere or not.

The difference between a leader who operates from a place of love versus one who doesn't is whether or not they can put their own ego aside to exercise care and compassion, not just in the moment but throughout their working relationship with themselves and others. And yes, we can still make a living while being loving and compassionate. Dr. Moore writes that when motivated by love, "My desire to generate material wealth would lead me to ask myself 'how can I create more social value for others?' This love-induced economy allows me to see myself as an integral part of a larger community and to recognize that my well-being is dependent on the well-being of others (including the environment). The wealth I create is not grounded in the exploitation of others (workers/consumers) or the environment, and I can enjoy it without fear."[87] Leadership led by love is letting go of unrealistic expectations and perfection in order to be empathetic and compassionate toward ourselves, and those who are willingly on our team. By being the main example of love made visible to ourselves, our managers, and our provisionary team players (contractors and employees alike), we set the tone for a culture that is intolerable of shame and blame. We are the first to embody the policies we ask others to honor.

Therefore, when we read about policies like, "hire slow and fire fast" we won't misconstrue them in order to fit a twisted agenda fueled by passive-aggressive nature, narcissism, workplace codependency, or fear. With the foundation of a love ethic, we understand why it's important to take a thorough approach to adding provisions (i.e. recognition of leadership or creativity) to the company vision. Thorough means a structured process (one that's been developed with care and ahead of time) that ensures culture and work description fit, while at the same time having a checks and balances system embedded in the process to cover things like unconscious hiring bias. Many ways exist to accomplish that goal, including apps like Blendoor, created by startup founder Stephanie Lampkin, who saw a diversity and inclusion problem in companies and wanted to create a fair process for all prospective teammates.[88] And if need be, we mindfully let go. Mindfully letting go starts with the hiring process, continues with leadership leading by example and reiterating policies and expectations ... and not taking the lazy approach to abruptly ending a relationship because it's too troublesome for you to treat someone like a human rather than another cog in your moneymaking machine. This is a lot of upfront work; work that takes effort, responsibility, and accountability … work that makes subtle yet big differences.

CHECKS AND BALANCES SYSTEM AKA ACCOUNTABILITY.

I am personally torn about the concept of work-life balance because so many people define it in so many ways. Entrepreneurs think there is no place for it in the startup climate, and business owners wonder if they can actually have it and survive. I firmly believe we can compartmentalize the dealings of our lives for only so long before it infiltrates into our work or at the very least our attitudes about either the work or the people we work with. Yet too much work-life integration blurs the lines. With that being said, we're human and sometimes we allow people into our lives who are meant to teach us lessons and help us grow, mainly because we end up needing the patience of the biblical character Job to keep from pulling out our hair around them. And that too requires self-compassion because the truth is, when in a situation that has you second-guessing yourself and wondering about the value of your worth (something that happens to the best of us as employees, as startup founders, CEOs and as business owners), it is necessary to take a step back to reevaluate your values, standards, and wellbeing. But who has time to take a step back and do an analysis when you're running a business? That's why love takes effort. And accountability goes a long way to ensure you dot i's and cross t's. This starts with being accountable to yourself, and by accepting responsibility for how you lead, which includes your vision and how you expected that vision to manifest.

If we are building a workplace culture for which we've decided to first sacrifice much in order to achieve success – no matter the means – and then once we have enough material success, then we'll concern ourselves with things like wellness, love and compassion. Well, what kind of organization are we really building when we use whatever materials we happen to have left to spare? How much of our pure intentions get lost by playing the game to win in order to destroy the game? This answer to all this is perhaps not an easy pill to digest. There isn't even a one answer that fits all this line of questioning. But we do have thought starters that may give us an *aha!* I'll share one with you:

> *If what we're practicing now is running ourselves into the ground … at what point will we practice something different? Because whatever we practice now is what we will practice in the future… What we need is the combination of a mind that wants to change the world and a mind that is steady, clear-seeing, and seeks change from a place of love…*[89] *– angel Kyodo Williams*

Because you can so easily to lose sight of the "whys" when so wrapped up in the day-to-day "whats" and "hows" to make a buck, it is very important to surround yourself with your own version of the *three* wise men or wise women.

- First are people who will love you for you as a person, not just because of your title or bank account. These are the kind of people who will speak life over your soul and tell you about yourself when you're out of control.
- Next are the individuals who will help you think outside of the confines of your own self-imposed box of limitations, like a therapist, coach, or mentor.
- Finally, there are the people who are amazing at what they do in order to help you see *your* vision through, including: your

right-hand woman; specialty contractors; COO; app developers; housekeeper; and childcare provider.

All three types of wise individuals will help you with balance; ultimately, though, it is you who must remain firm in your resolve to be the change you want to see in your company and life.

UNAPOLOGETIC WOMAN WHO HAPPENS TO BE A BUSINESS OWNER, AND AN ADVOCATE FOR MENTAL WELLNESS.

For a long time, I had been uncomfortably numb, but numb was all I knew how to be and I didn't believe girls like me got much better out of life. I grew up to have a mindset of constantly settling. I'd find some courage through someone else's eyes and vision for my life and run with it before all came tumbling right back down. I took this way of life into my interpersonal relationships and as a result avoided people as much as possible, because I knew from history that once I welcomed them into my life, into my emotional space, I would not like the person I would become around them. The abandonment issues of my past, and the trauma from being gaslighted, kept me bound and I simply couldn't tolerate myself around anyone if they got too close. I knew I couldn't completely avoid people in business so it transformed and I carried the mentality with me when it came to my own business development and ongoing growth. An ounce of courage through someone else's faith, a state of perpetually being stuck, and wondering if I'd ever be good enough to simply support myself.

I hated these traits, thoughts, behavior patterns. One day I realized I needed to own it, this way of *not* being. I needed to breathe it in, to see myself from outside myself so I could finally forgive and show myself compassion. Like a beloved gazing down at a sleeping lover with unbridled kindness and unlimited love expecting nothing in return, I had to see myself as I am. Then, I had to start where I was. What was revealed was that I could not get out of this personal twilight zone on my own not without guidance, support, and boatloads of patience.

Whenever I think about the optimal health of a person and the culture groups of people create, I feel it is much like that symbolic meaning behind project semicolon: it's a journey, a process. Acceptance … real, unapologetic acceptance comes after you can really see yourself in action throughout that process. I say unapologetic because change hurts; it doesn't feel good when you are used to things and people fitting into your neat box topped with saran wrap and it's going to take an unapologetic approach to stepping up and doing what's best for you.

Likewise, we'll have to take an unapologetic approach to creating long-lasting shifts in the way we conduct business. By actively working toward transforming workplace cultures to be purposed for something that contributes to outward expressions of love made visible, we step into a new dimension of entrepreneurship. We must become *"purposepreneurs."*

When asked to share some wisdom nuggets about purposefully addressing mental and emotional health issues on the road to becoming a successful business woman, this what my interview participants had to share.

I had to shift my mindset about success. To me, business is no longer about a conventional success; it's about building a sustainable life and business that accommodates my mental health needs. – "Jane"

Watch out for perfectionism. If we start looking at failure as something beautiful and success as much more than instant gratification, we can move through changes in due season. It takes time to find out what's going to work for you and your business. It takes a lot of trial and error. – "Amaya"

Honesty is often misconstrued as negativity. If we can't have candid and honest conversations how can we ever build a cohesive culture? Even before that, self-evaluation is so important. If you don't know who you are or your values, you will literally sell your soul to the devil. Sure, I have been duped and cheated. But I realized you can be angry and stay bitter about failed investments or you can be willing to forgive yourself for taking the okey-doke, forgive them, learn from your past and keep it moving. – "Tia"

Entrepreneurs don't like listening to directions that's why it may be more helpful for us to have something like a symposium where can openly talk about this and hear from leadership we admire and respect who are willing to share their stories. It is true entrepreneurs are a different breed, but we believe that we're so unique that we hold ourselves back from asking for help. – "Eleanor"

Stop comparing ourselves to perfectly manicured profiles of what a business owner looks like. People aren't talking about struggles and we need to do more of that to paint a realistic picture. – "Willow"

GIVE MEANING TO YOUR BUSINESS THROUGH THE MESSAGE OF YOUR LIFE, WORK ETHICS, AND POLICIES.

Purpose is truly the journey of a lifetime. I think pursuing our practical life purposes can feel especially daunting when you are in the midst of specific triggers that eventually set you on a path toward mental and emotional health issues. The original causes of our spiraling out of control emotions and breakdowns vary. Is it a chemical imbalance? Is it a lack of love? I believe I've properly exposed you to just enough data to suggest how these issues are a bit of both and so much more. But as leaders we are not here to get wrapped up in embracing labels; we are here to be pioneers and break glass ceilings. We are here to step up to the plate and be what we felt was lacking in the market place ... we are here to show the way.

Leaders are indeed in a unique position. They have higher calling just the same as everyone else; however, they are able to carry out that calling as the captain of their own ships where people have decided to come aboard. They have the opportunity to remind people under their governance that they matter and to even inspire them to be captains of their own purposed arenas. How great are leaders who sees the wonderful gifts of the people on their teams? How much more are we willing to continue a simple contact and turn it into a *"real-lationship,"* where we give the rapport building some real effort, knowing it yields better results? How much better equipped are we when engaging relationally with one another, instead of treating each other like a transaction? There is such a need for compassionate captains who put in a great deal of effort to prevent good crew members from drowning because they haven't yet learned how to swim.

C O N C L U S I O N

IF WE ARE GOING TO present the notion that we are to be trusted, that we are to be mentors, advisors, and visionaries, and hold the livelihood of others in our hands – then it is our responsibility and honor to actively cultivate what we need in order to be the most authentic versions of ourselves as much, and as often as possible.

If we are blessed enough to have awakened, or be "woke," then I think it's only fair to guide others toward doing the same, and in such a way that best represents our unique outward expression of transformational love.

I believe we are all born with the right tools to solve any problems we face in life, but socialization teaches us fear while ego introduces us to oppression, so we forget where we've placed those tools and how to use them. However, for every bump and twist in the road, we gain opportunities to find ourselves if we really want to know who we truly are and what we are really capable of. We have the choice to perceive our circumstances as hopeless destinations, or the motivational force to strive for a destiny we have the power to create. "Turn your mess into your message" is a way of manifesting love in the world through our work. If we can remain ever resilient – taking perceived failures as lessons to uncover and unleash our hidden strengths, our unique superpowers, I believe we can and will make a difference and even legitimately change the world.

Because love made visible is energy we can all put into the universe, through consistent and persistent effort we will yield tangible results. However, to transform energy in the direction of health and wellness is not a one-woman initiative. It is a movement. One both women and men can get on board with. So, if you still need one, here is your official invitation to join this movement. **Visit www.loveselflovebiz.com to learn how you can get involved.**

I thank you in advance for your courage to lead with a foundation of love and in the direction of optimal health and wellness.

REFERENCES

———

1. Estés, C. P. (1992). *Women who run with the wolves: Myths and stories of the wild woman archetype.* New York: Ballantine Books.

2. Freeman, M.A., Johnson, S.L., Staudenmaier, P.J., & Zisser, M.R. (2015). *Are Entrepreneurs "Touched with Fire".* Retrieved from MichaelFreemanmd.com: http://www.michaelafreeman-md.com/Research.html

3. Peers, J., Bennett, G. Booth, G. (1979). *1,001 Logical Laws, Accurate Axioms, Profound Principles* (p. 85). Doubleday & Company, Inc., Garden City, New York.

4. World Health Organization [WHO]. (n.d.). *Mental health: A state of well-being.* Retrieved June 22, 2017, from http://www.who.int/features/factfiles/mental_health/en/

5. Fosley, G, Jr., Wachs, R.D. (Producers), & Landis, J. (Director). (1988). *Coming to America* [Motion picture]. United States: Paramount Pictures.

6. Success (2017). In Merriam-webster.com. Retrieved from https://www.merriam-webster.com/dictionary/success

7. Jamison, K. R. (1996). *Touched with fire: Manic-depressive illness and the artistic temperament.* New York: Free Press Paperbacks, Published by Simon & Schuster.

8. Ghaemi, S. N. (2012). *A first-rate madness: Uncovering the links between leadership and mental illness.* New York: Penguin Books.

9. Freeman, M.A., Johnson, S.L., Staudenmaier, P.J., & Zisser, M.R. (2015). *Are Entrepreneurs "Touched with Fire".* Retrieved from MichaelFreemanmd.com: http://www.michaelafreeman-md.com/Research.html

10. Freeman, M.A., Johnson, S.L., Staudenmaier, P.J., & Zisser, M.R. (2015). *Are Entrepreneurs "Touched with Fire".* Retrieved from MichaelFreemanmd.com: http://www.michaelafreeman-md.com/Research.html

11. The Money and Mental Health Policy Institute. (2017, February 17). *Saving lives with money advice.* Retrieved June 22, 2017, from http://www.moneyandmentalhealth.org/saving-lives-with-money-advice/

12. Guillebeau, C. (2012). The $100 startup: *How to fire your boss and create a new future.* London: Macmillan.

13. American Express OPEN. (2016) *Sixth Annual State of Women Owned Business Report.* Retrieved June 22, 2017, from http://

about.americanexpress.com/news/pr/2016/2016-state-of-women-owned-business.aspx

14. National Women's Business Council. (n.d.). *Women-owned Businesses* [Fact sheet]. Retrieved June 22, 2017, from https://www.nwbc.gov/facts/women-owned-businesses

15. National Women's Business Council. (n.d.). *Women-owned Businesses* [Fact sheet]. Retrieved June 22, 2017, from https://www.nwbc.gov/facts/women-owned-businesses

16. Brown, J., & Newsome, B.J. (1966). *It's a Man's Man's Man's World* [Recorded by J. Brown]. On It's a Man's Man's Man's World [Vinyl record]. New York, NY: King Records.

17. Gao, G. (2015, May 08). *Americans' ideal family size is smaller than it used to be.* Retrieved June 22, 2017, from http://www.pewresearch.org/fact-tank/2015/05/08/ideal-size-of-the-american-family/

18. Allen, P. (1997). *The Concept of Woman, Volume 1: The Aristotelian Revolution, 750 B.C. - A. D. 1250.* Grand Rapids, MI/ Cambridge, U.K.: Eerdmans

19. World Health Organization [WHO]. (n.d.). *Gender and women's mental health.* Retrieved June 22, 2017, from http://www.who.int/mental_health/prevention/genderwomen/en/

20. World Health Organization [WHO]. (February 2017). *Depression* [Fact sheet]. Retrieved June 22, 2017, from http://www.who.int/mediacentre/factsheets/fs369/en/

21. NAMI. (n.d.). *Risk Of Suicide.* Retrieved June 22, 2017, from https://www.nami.org/Learn-More/Mental-Health-Conditions/ Related-Conditions/Suicide

22. Harvard Health Publications. (May 2011). *Women and depression.* Retrieved June 22, 2017, from http://www.health.harvard.edu/ womens-health/women-and-depression

23. Vitti, A. (2014). *Woman code: Perfect your cycle, amplify your fertility, supercharge your sex drive, and become a power source.* New York, NY: HarperOne, an imprint of HarperCollins.

24. Friedlander, J. (2013). *Business from bed: The 6-step comeback plan to get yourself working again after a health crisis.* New York, NY: Demos Health Pub.

25. Phillips J., Jacobs, S., & Styles, D. (1997-1998). *Money, Power & Respect* [Recorded by The Lox]. On Money, Power & Respect [Vinyl, CD]. New York, NY: Bad Boy Records.

26. Pratt, L.A. Ph.D., Brody, D.J., M.P.H., and Gu, Q M.D., Ph.D. (2011, October 19). *Antidepressant Use in Persons Aged 12 and Over: United States, 2005–2008.* Retrieved June 22, 2017, from https://www.cdc.gov/nchs/data/data-briefs/db76.htm

27. Friedlander, J. (2013). *Business from bed: The 6-step comeback plan to get yourself working again after a health crisis.* New York, NY: Demos Health Pub.

28. Michalowicz, M. (2008). *The toilet paper entrepreneur: The tell-like-it-is guide to cleaning up in business, even if you are at the end of your roll.* Bontoon, NJ: Obsidian Launch, LLC.

29. Sinek, S. (2013). *Start with why: How great leaders inspire everyone to take action.* London: Portfolio/Penguin.

30. Moltz, B. J. (2008). *You need to be a little crazy: The truth about starting and growing your business.* Bloomington, IN: AuthorHouse.

31. Freeman, M.A., Johnson, S.L., Staudenmaier, P.J., & Zisser, M.R. (2015). *Are Entrepreneurs "Touched with Fire".* Retrieved from MichaelFreemanmd.com: http://www.michaelafreeman-md.com/Research.html

32. Freeman, M.A., Johnson, S.L., Staudenmaier, P.J., & Zisser, M.R. (2015). *Are Entrepreneurs "Touched with Fire".* Retrieved from MichaelFreemanmd.com: http://www.michaelafreeman-md.com/Research.html

33. Smith, W., Black, T., Blumenthal, J., Lassiter, J. & Tisch, S. (Producers), & Muccino, G. (Director). (2006). *The Pursuit of Happyness* [Motion picture]. United States: Columbia Pictures.

34. Gerber, M. E. (2014). *The e-myth revisited: Why most small businesses don't work and what to do about it.* New York, NY: Harper Business.

35. Fromm, E. (1942). *The fear of freedom.* London: Routledge & Kegan Paul.

36. Callender, K. (2013). The Serenity Prayer. Psych Central. Retrieved on August 1, 2017, from https://blogs.psychcentral.com/lessons/2013/06/the-serenity-prayer/

37. Webinars That Convert. (n.d.). Webinars That Convert, AmyPorterfield.com. Retrieved from www.amyporterfield.com/webinarsthatconvert/.

38. Rosie the Riveter. (n.d.). In Wikipedia. Retrieved June 22, 2017, from https://en.wikipedia.org/wiki/Rosie_the_Riveter

39. Lorde, Audre. (1988). *A burst of light: essays.* Ithaca, N.Y.: Firebrand Books

40. Brown, B. (2010). *The Gifts of Imperfection: Let go of who you think you're supposed to be and embrace who you are.* Center City, Minnesota: Hazeldon.

41. Stiles, P. (2008). *Working Paper Series the Negative Side of Motivation: the Role of Shame.* Retrieved from https://www.semanticscholar.org/paper/Working-Paper-Series-the-Negative-Side-of-Motivati-Stiles/4757e3c1a5c0cc0a13da5a66eadfa92da7e469c8

42. Arylo, C. (2012). *Madly in love with me: The daring adventure of becoming your own best friend.* California: New World Library.

43. Collins, S. (2008). *The Hunger Games.* New York: Scholastic Press.

44. Stigma (2017). In OxfordDictionaries.com. Retrieved from https://en.oxforddictionaries.com/definition/stigma

45. NAMI: National Alliance on Mental Illness. (n.d.). *Risks of suicide.* Retrieved June 22, 2017, from https://www.nami.org/Learn-More/ Mental-Health-Conditions/Related-Conditions/Suicide

46. Caruso, K. Suicide.org. (n.d.). *Suicide Causes.* Retrieved June 22, 2017, from http://www.suicide.org/suicide-causes.html

47. NAMI: National Alliance on Mental Illness. (n.d.). *Risks of suicide.* Retrieved June 22, 2017, from https://www.nami.org/ Learn-More/Mental-Health-Conditions/Related-Conditions/ Suicide

48. World Health Organization [WHO]. (February 2017). *Depression* [Fact sheet]. Retrieved June 22, 2017, from http://www.who.int/ mediacentre/factsheets/fs369/en/

49. The Anxiety and Depression Association of America (ADAA). (n.d.). *Depression.* [Fact sheet]. Retrieved June 22, 2017, from https://www.adaa.org/understanding-anxiety/depression/

50. Waters, R. (1972-1973). *Money* [Recorded by Pink Floyd]. On The Dark Side of the Moon. [Vinyl]. Westminster, London, England: Harvest Records.

51. The Money and Mental Health Policy Institute. (2016). *Money and Mental Health: The Facts.* [Fact sheet]. Retrieved June 22, 2017, from http://www.moneyandmentalhealth.org/facts/

52. American Foundation for Suicide Prevention. (2015). *Suicide Statistics — AFSP.* Retrieved June 22, 2017, from https://afsp. org/about-suicide/suicide-statistics/

53. Estés, C. P. (1992). *Women who run with the wolves: Myths and stories of the wild woman archetype*. New York: Ballantine Books.

54. Moore, T. (2015). *A religion of one's own: A guide to creating a personal spirituality in a secular world*. New York: Avery, an imprint of Penguin Random House.

55. Hughes, L. (1969). *Not without laughter*. New York: Collier Books.

56. Angelou, Maya. (1969). *I know why the caged bird sings*. New York: Random House.

57. American Foundation for Suicide Prevention. (n.d.). *A Model School Policy on Suicide Prevention- AFSP*. Retrieved June 22, 2017, from https://afsp.org/our-work/education/model-school-policy-suicide-prevention/

58. Brown, B. (2008). *I thought it was just me (but it isn't): Making the journey from "what will people think?" to "I am enough"*. New York: Gotham Books.

59. Shorey, H. (2015, April 19). *Fear of Intimacy and Closeness in Relationships*. Retrieved June 22, 2017, from https://www.psychologytoday.com/blog/the-freedom-change/201504/fear-intimacy-and-closeness-in-relationships

60. Mandela, N. (1995). *Long walk to freedom: The autobiography of Nelson Mandela*. Boston: Back Bay Books.

61. Brown, B. (2010). *The gifts of imperfection: Let go of who you think you're supposed to be and embrace who you are.* Center City, Minn.: Hazelden.

62. Harvard Health Publications (October 2015). *Going off anti-depressants.* Retrieved June 22, 2017, from http://www.health.harvard.edu/diseases-and-conditions/going-off-antidepressants

63. American Psychological Association. (n.d.). *The road to resilience.* Retrieved June 22, 2017, from http://www.apa.org/helpcenter/road-resilience.aspx

64. [TEDx Talks]. (2013, April 12). *Chimamanda Ngozi Adichie: We should all be feminists* [Video File]. Retrieved from https://www.youtube.com/watch?v=hg3umXU_qWc

65. Edmunds, K.B. (1995). *My love, sweet love* [Recorded by Patti LaBelle]. On Waiting to Exhale: Original Soundtrack Album [Compact Disc]. New York, NY: Arista Records.

66. [James Wright Chanel]. (2015, November 12). *My review on Patti LaBelle sweet potato pie review.* [Video File]. Retrieved from https://youtu.be/eQRwFn7WPk8

67. [Lady Gaga]. (2017, April 17). *Lady Gaga + Prince William | Heads Together | #oktosay* [Video File]. Retrieved from https://www.youtube.com/watch?v=73WmwtJM-50

68. Lennon, J. (1967). *All you need is love* [Recorded by The Beatles] [Vinyl]. London, England: Parlophone Records.

69. John, E. (2013). Love is the cure: On life, loss, and the end of AIDS. New York: Back Bay Books.

70. Ladinski, D. (2002). *Love poems from God: Twelve sacred voices from the East and West.* New York: Penguin Compass.

71. Silver, J. (Producer), & The Wachowskis, (Directors). (1999). *The Matrix* [Motion picture]. United States: Warner Bros.

72. Mendel, B. (Producer), & Whedon J. (Director). (2005). *Serenity* [Motion picture]. United States: Universal Pictures.

73. Cure (2017). In OxfordDictionaries.com. Retrieved from https://en.oxforddictionaries.com/definition/cure

74. Care (2017). In OxfordDictionaries.com. Retrieved from https://en.oxforddictionaries.com/definition/care

75. Concern (2017). In OxfordDictionaries.com. Retrieved from https://en.oxforddictionaries.com/definition/concern

76. Responsibility (2017). In OxfordDictionaries.com. Retrieved from https://en.oxforddictionaries.com/definition/responsibility

77. Peck, M. S. (2003). *The road less traveled: A new psychology of love, traditional values and spiritual growth.* New York: Simon & Schuster.

78. Peck, M. S. (2003). *The road less traveled: A new psychology of love, traditional values and spiritual growth.* New York: Simon & Schuster.

79. Hooks, B. (2000). *All about love: New visions*. New York: Harper Perennial.

80. Moore, K. (2016). *Your Life As A Celebration: Accomplishing your goals with less stress and more joy* Kindle Edition. Butterfly Productions. Retrieved June 22, 2017, from https://www. amazon.com/Your-Life-As-Celebration-Accomplishing-ebook/ dp/B01KECDB0O

81. [Mindfulness Academy Scandinavia]. (2015 April, 5). *Mindfulness - An introduction with Jon Kabat-Zinn* [Video File]. Retrieved from https://youtu.be/xeCXhXDkzpw

82. Gallup. (2011-2012). *State of the Global Workplace*. Retrieved from http://www.gallup.com/services/178517/state-global-workplace. aspx

83. Cook, J. (n.d.). American Society of Association Executives™ (ASAE). *The Benefits of Workplace Wellness Programs*. Retrieved June 22, 2017, from https://www. asaecenter.org/resources/articles/an_magazine/2012/july/ the-benefits-of-workplace-wellness-programs

84. Conner D. (2010, February 23). *Resilience in Teams and Organizations*. Retrieved June 22, 2017, from http:// www.connerpartners.com/frameworks-and-processes/ resilience-in-teams-and-organizations

85. The Institute for Research on Unlimited Love. (n.d.). *Love Suffused Work*. Retrieved June 22, 2017, from http://unlimited-loveinstitute.org/newsletter/triner-love-suffused-work.php

86. Fromm, E. (1967). *The art of loving.* New York: Bantam Books.

87. Moore, K. (2016). *Your Life As A Celebration: Accomplishing your goals with less stress and more joy* Kindle Edition. Butterfly Productions. Retrieved June 22, 2017, from https://www.amazon.com/Your-Life-As-Celebration-Accomplishing-ebook/dp/B01KECDB0O

88. Davis, L. (2016). *Be The Change Series Interviews - Featuring: Stephanie Lampkin.* Retrieved June 22, 2017, from http://lynette-davis.com/2016/08/16/be-the-change-stephanie-lampkin/

89. Williams, A.K. & Salzberg, S. (2017, March 15). *Love Everyone: A Guide for Spiritual Activists.* Retrieved June 23, 2017, from https://www.lionsroar.com/love-everyone-a-guide-for-spiritual-activists/

ACKNOWLEDGMENTS

———

The real VIPS are the courageous women and men who responded to my request to share their knowledge and experience. I cannot even begin to explain how honored I feel, to be granted access to such delicate pieces of their stories. I am forever grateful for the life-changing wisdom I received just from listening. I pray I did their revelations some justice.

This was truly a project of love and I could not have done it without my collaborative partnerships – many of whom are the subject matter experts quoted in the book. To the people who made this book possible – and this includes all of the amazing authors who've written excellent works that have planted seeds of growth in me – I thank you.

To my miracle-working book editor, Pamela Barroway, thank you for your patience and care. To my photographer Jeff Lek, illustrator Susan Krupp, and book design team, thank you for bringing everything together and making a beautiful product. To my amazing team: my administrator, Darlene, and my web copy editor, Autumn – you ladies rock! I am so thankful to have had your support on various projects over the years. To the amazing business coaches I've worked with throughout this process: Kyna, Jennie, Shenee, Brandy, and

Anastacia. I am grateful for your guidance, and humbled by the growing pains you've encouraged me through.

A special thanks to Sara and my fellow PowerMatch members for the push to take #loveselflovebiz to the next level. To Jardana and Amanda, thanks for keeping me on track and on purpose as my accountability partners. Also, Audrey, Deborah, and Jana – ladies, you went above and beyond to offer resources and support and I can't thank you enough! Another special thanks to Ryan, Rachael, and Sara G., for coming through for me whenever I had website difficulties. Likewise, I am so very grateful to my advance copy book reviewers. Thank you for your honest feedback and support during the book launch. Last but not least I want to thank all of my Facebook friends who voted on the original cover design and gave me feedback and well-wishes on the book.

To my clients. Thank you for partnering with me. If it wasn't for your willingness to take a chance on me; your faith in my possibilities; and your trust in my ability to get 'er done, I would not have had the space to create.

When I lamented about how I couldn't do this and how I should wait until I retire to write, my family was there. I wanted to give up but there they were telling me I can do this, telling how proud they were of me, supporting me, praying for me, loving me. Thank you to my Mamu, my Grammy Pammy, Kimberly "li'l sis," Nathiel "brother," and Marlon "bro-bro" too! Thank you for bringing into my life my sister-in-loves, and my wonderful nieces and nephews who teach me patience every single time I hear a crash and boom. My aunties, uncles, and cousins – I thank you all too. This poem is for each and every one of you:

I know who we are, we have journeyed so very far
Still, I hear this call, it beckons me, it knows me by my name

I carry us beyond the seas of shattered dreams and graves of sorrow
The hope of yesteryears, when courage laughs in the face of fears
I know who we are, I carry us all inside me

I am truly blessed to have so many amazing women and men in my life, but I do want to acknowledge my dearest friends who offered me so much support, encouragement, and kindness during the process of writing this book. Latisha "Tish," Josh, P. Elizabeth, and Semonna. To Vernetta, Sabrina, Nava, C.J., and Dave thank you for that much needed quality time.

To Dierra, Nathaniel "Marc," and Aletha thank you for being my shelter during the storm. To Kathy Meline, M.Ed., Anita Novembre, M.Ed., and of course Vince DiPasquale, M.A. for helping me heal my inner child and activate my inner superheroine. And to all of my recovery family at the Starting Point and beyond, thank you for reminding me that I am not alone.

I could go on forever and day about all the amazing women in my life, but I'd need a whole book to write about them all. So, I'll leave it at this: Ladies, you inspire me, you invigorate me, you encourage me to be the best me I can be, and I am so very truly blessed to have known you. Whether our season has come and gone or we still enjoy each other's company today, I love you, my sisters.

LYNETTE DAVIS IS A MENTAL health peer advocate who writes, organizes events, and facilitates conversations centered on holistic wellness. Her articles, poetry, and "old-soul" wisdom has been featured in local magazines, blogs, an award-winning tour, and several podcasts. She created the *Love Yourself Love Your Business* initiative as a hub of collaborated projects to get business owners, entrepreneurs, and professionals mindful about mental health and actively engaged in wholehearted activities that foster wellness in and out of the workplace. She lives in southern New Jersey. Visit the author online at www.loveselflovebiz.com.

9 781974 608911